The Key to Vegetarianism and Health
Made Plain and Simple

"Health is your greatest wealth"

John Truitte

By
John Truitte
AKA
Adewole Babafemi

Published by

TEACH Services, Inc.
Box 254, Donovan Road
Brushton, New York 12916

Dedicated to, and in memory of
Jerome Creecy and my late brother Mark Truitte

Contents

FORWARD vi

INTRODUCTION ix

BLACK AND BROWN PEOPLES 1

WHICH WAY IS UP? 3

      a.) Types Of Vegetarians 3

      b.) Nutrient Composition of the Body 4

      c.) General Classifications of Foods 5

      d.) Desirable Height-Weight Relation 7

      e.) Factors Affecting the Digestive Processes 8

      f.) Food Combination Charts 10

HEALTHFUL TIPS 15

WATER 19

FRUITS AND VEGETABLES 23

FREE RADICALS AND OPPONENTS 27

BREAD 31

CHEESE 33

SUGAR 37

MINERALS 41

VITAMINS 49

SUBSTANCES THAT ROB THE BODY OF NUTRIENTS 58

HERBS FOR COOKING, BAKING & SALADS 62

      a.) Herbal Remedies 65

      b.) Minerals and Vitamin Sources of Herbs 70

      c.) Herbal Tips 75

FLOWER POLLEN 77

BEE PROPOLIS 85

BEAUTY HINTS 89

DISEASES 93

ENVIRONMENTAL TOXINS 97

Forward

As a physician, when counseling patients regarding weight reduction, I emphasize reduction in caloric intake and exercise. Both of these seem simple but are hard to apply and require self-discipline and motivation. Unfortunately, most people look for the quick or easy fix (the popularity of 'diet pills' is an example).

In devoting our attention to weight reduction we have, in general, failed to acknowledge a more important implication of the food intake: the effect of food on health and longevity. The world can be characterized by the 'haves' and 'have nots.' The former usually die because of what they have and the latter die because of what they do not have. The medical community now, more than ever, understands the importance of food and its influence on our general well-being.

Many diseases of a civilized society can be directly related to the nature of its food consumption. Diverticulosis, coronary artery disease, adult-onset diabetes mellitus, high blood pressure, and, as recent investigations suggest, some malignancies (cancers) can be correlated with long-term food habits.

Disease can be confusing. As we are well aware, every one in a community does not become ill during an epidemic. Even the plague of the fourteenth century, which killed nearly 20 million people or almost one in five of the inhabitants of Europe at that time, had its survivors, and this was before the era of antibiotics, immunization, quarantine, disease surveillance, and public health and hygiene. Specific immune traits probably determined the survivors of the plague, at least those that were exposed to the offending agent. Those immunity traits may or may not have been hereditary. Since the mass utilization of genetic analysis and DNA recombinant techniques, it has become easier to perform intricate genetic analysis. Although still in its infancy, this analysis can identify individuals who might be susceptible to certain diseases. With some diseases, the presence or absence of certain genes can promote or prevent the disease under certain environmental conditions, which can be conditions related to food intake or external environmental factors.

We have all heard the comment that two individuals can eat the same foods yet one gains weight and the other doesn't. This is further amplified with cholesterol levels in which two individuals with similar eating habits can have cholesterol values that differ by more than two hundred points (one normal, the other seriously elevated).

What are we to do? The whole area is confusing and changing every day, for new information is constantly being added to the knowledge base. Unfortunately, the reports are sometimes conflicting: one day coffee is bad for us because it can cause cancer; another day, coffee is good for us. If we just bounced from fad to fad or report to report there would be no significant gain in the long-term. As in the stock market, it is persistence with a few good basic strategies that pays off in the long-term. SO it is with food selection. Let's settle on a few basics. Forget about trying to loose weight; think about overall health, and, maybe, the weight will take care of itself, especially if exercise is included; but that is another issue.

Whether we like it or not, man/woman is a member of the animal kingdom. Each living organism on this planet lives by consuming another living organism, be it a plant or non-plant organism. The energy transferred is not directly related to the size of the consumer nor the size of the consumed (note that the organisms consumed by whales are small compared to the enormous size of whales). Another interesting contrast is the following: the enormous size and strength of elephants are fueled by diets free of meat products or animal matter. Human beings appear to be the only creatures whose diet can interfere with their bodies' normal function. Scientifically, other factors, some of which have been eluded to, are involved, but Mr. Truitte, in his book, approaches the diet issue as a simple question of meat versus non-meat. With over 230 years of experience in nutrition and herbal medicine he presents an easy path to eating for health and longevity. Through my spouse, I have been the recipient of many health fad diets over the past years. During one interval, surprisingly, I had been on a vegetarian diet for nearly four weeks before realizing that we had not had any real meat. Before that revelation, the idea of repeated meals without meat was not palatable. As Mr. Truitte clearly reveals, there is nothing complicated nor mysterious about being a vegetarian; it is certainly palatable. In today's climate of health consciousness, it even has a level of respect and admiration. Many restaurants now have vegetarian entrees; conventions or seminars/meetings even allow for the potential presence of vegetarians at their luncheons. The main point, especially for those who feel that giving up meat is a sacrifice in cuisine, is that the absence of meat is not a sacrifice. There is plenty of meat-less food out there waiting to be consumed! Enjoy Mr. Truitte's explorations in the cuisine of vegetarianism; he explains the sometimes misunderstood different approaches to vegetarianism and provides information, sometimes controversial, regarding the direct application of food substances for healing. In general, Mr. Truitte's book is delightful and provides a pathway toward wonderful cuisine and, hopefully, improved health and longevity.

James Dorsey, M.D.,FRCSC

Acknowledgments

In acknowledgement of my beloved sister, Linda Truitte...

and with special thanks to some of the men and women whom I've known and communicated with over the years and who have inspired me to be a Vegetarian, such as Dick Gregory, Alvena Fulton, Gary Null, Viktoras Kulvinskas, Elijah Muhammad, Seventh Day Adventist Church, Donald Thomas, Kanya, Dr. John Moore, Ms. Blackman, Eileen, Mrs. Charles, Frank & Dr. Patricia Spradley, Cliff Kitching, Fadhilika Atiba-Weza, James Dorsey M.D., John and Jessie Truitte, Wanique, Tony, Lloyd, Verlette Green (Ife), Delores McCullough, Samuel Salisbury, H.B. Miller, K.C., and my son Kerry Porter. I would also like to thank Barbara Roseboro for her typing and Oswald Gift for his vision.

Introduction

This book was written in an attempt to raise the level of consciousness in health and nutrition. It behooves me to see the premature aging of our children, due to the exploits of Burger King, McDonald's and Kentucky Fried Chicken, etc., for there are many growth hormones, chemicals and antibiotics that are routinely administered in animals. These agents in meat are the cause of children and adults to look older than their ages, as a result of excessive amounts of these aforementioned agents in meat. It is true that we are what we eat, however, we become what we eat. The food that we eat, the drugs that we ingest debilitate our human and spiritual potential, and there are many untapped resources in herbs, flowers and plant life, that can contribute to the make up of human behavior and development.

In some African American communities, cigarette and alcohol advertisements, along with fast food chains are deliberately targeted at African Americans, because they are the biggest buyers and consumers of these products. African American women are the largest group in America, that are smokers, especially teenagers.

Soft drinks, such as Mountain Dew, contain the highest amounts of caffeine, more than other commercial soft drinks, such as Pepsi and Coco-Cola. Freshly squeezed fruit and vegetable juice are body enhancers, for growth and development. The public though, is conned in believing that their thirst is quenched by these same soft drinks, which can cause osteoporosis, hypoglycemia, in addition to which the harmful effects of acids in soda soften the enamel on the teeth. The combination of sugar and acids provide a medium for bacteria to develop cavities. Excessive consumption of sodas can even cause cirrhosis of the liver, even in young children, similar to the effects of alcohol on the liver.

Environmental toxins such as electromagnetic radiation, from color televisions, microwave ovens, video terminals, etc., contribute to various forms of cancer and tumors. There are also chemicals in tap water that can cause children to become mentally lethargic, as a result of the lead content in tap water, along with other chemicals. The high cholesterol contents of eggs, cheese and other dairy products, contribute to various heart diseases and migraine headaches.

To establish a basic premise for health is my primary reason for writing this book. May the love that is given to us by nature, be acknowledged in the way we learn to love ourselves, so let us submit to the will of nature, and be that example in what, where, and how we eat to live.

John Truitte 4/13/93

BLACK AND BROWN PEOPLES

Black and brown people should always eat foods from tropical climate, especially foods grown on or around the equator.

"African people and other colored races that live on the equatorial area were raised for centuries on tropical equatorial plants. In fact, Africans' diets consisted of tropical vegetation for 100,000 to 200,000 years before invasions by other races. Biologically, the stomach flora (friendly germs, bacteria, fungus, yeast, and virus) has not changed in Black folks' stomachs. It will take 2,000 years for the flora in Black folks' stomachs to change. This causes Blacks to digest tropical plants easier and will balance blacks metabolically. Consequently, tropical plants are the best stabilizers of an African holistic diet. Furthermore, tropical herbs are the best herbal medicines."

Llaila O. Afrika

WHICH WAY IS UP?

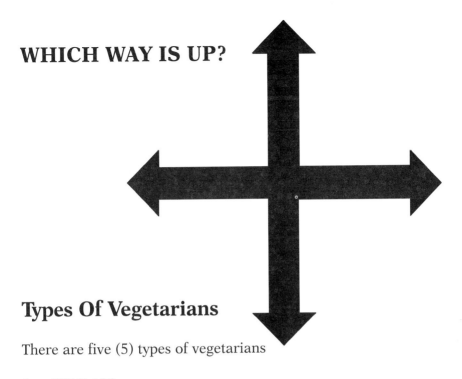

Types Of Vegetarians

There are five (5) types of vegetarians

1. **VEGAN:**

    As the strictest of vegetarians, this type rejects ALL animal foods, including meat, poultry, eggs, fish, dairy products and honey.

2. **LACTO-Vegetarians:**

    Drink milk and eat milk products in addition to vegetable foods.

3. **LACTO-OVO-Vegetarians:**

    Eat eggs, along with milk products and vegetables.

4. **PESCO-Vegetarians:**

    In addition to eating fish, plant and vegetables sources. In Asia, hundreds of millions of people follow this type of diet, living on staples of rice and fish.

5. **POLLO-Vegetarians:**

    Eat poultry, plant and vegetable sources, but they omit red meats from their diets.

Nutrient Composition of the Body

WATER	70%	WATER
PROTEIN	20%	PROTEIN
FAT	15%	FAT
MINERAL	5%	MINERAL
CARBOHYDRATE	2%	CARBOHYDRATE
VITAMINS	1%	VITAMINS

General Classifications of Foods

PROTEIN	GREEN and LOW STARCH VEGETABLES		STARCH
Almond	Asparagus	Mushroom	Beans:
Avocado	Bamboo Shoots	Mustard Greens	Red, White
Butternut	Beet Greens	Mustard Spinach	Pinto, Calico
Beechnut	Broccoli	Radish	Lima, Mung
Brazil Nut	Cabbage	Sweet Pepper	Chestnut
Cashew Nut	Cauliflower	Snap Beans	Corn
Filbert	Celery	Green Beans	Cowpeas
Hickory Nut	Chicory Greens	Okra	Potato
Lentils	Collards	Rhubarb	Rice
Olive	Chayote	Spinach	Sweet potato
Peanut	Cress	Summer Squash	Winter Squash:
Pignolia Nut	Cucumber	Yellow, Scallop	Acorn
Pilinut	Dock (Sorrel)	Cocozelle Zucchini	Butternut
Pinon Nut	Endive (Escarole)	Swiss Chard	Hubbard
Pumpkin Seed	Eggplant	Tomato	Peas
Safflower Seed	Fennel	Turnip	Taro Corms &
Soybean	Kale	Vine Spinach	Tubers
English Walnut	Kohlrabi	Watercress	Rye Grain
Black Walnut	Lettuce		Wheat Grain
	Mung Bean		Yam
	Sprouts		

ACID FRUIT	SUB-ACID FRUIT		SWEET FRUIT
Currant	Apple	Mango	Banana
Grapefruit	Apricot	Nectarine	Breadfruit
Kumquat	Blackberry	Papaya	Fig
Lemon	Cactus Fruit	Peach	Date
Lime	Cherimoya	Pear	Plantain
Loganberry	Cherry	Snap Beans	Raisin
Loquat	Elderberry	Persimmon	Dried Fruit
Orange	Gooseberry	Plum	Apple
Pineapple	Grapes	Quince	Pear
Pomegranate	Huckleberry	Sapodilla	Peach
Strawberry	JuJube	Sapota	Apricot
Tamarind			
Tangerine			

MELONS

Cantaloupe	Honeydew
Casaba	Nutmeg
Christmas	Persian
Cranshaw	Watermelon
Banana	

Desirable Height-Weight Relation

Height without shoes	WEIGHT in POUNDS (with indoor clothing)						
	MEN				WOMEN		
	Small Frame	Medium Frame	Large Frame		Small Frame	Medium Frame	Large Frame
4' 7"						94–104	102–116
8"					90–95	96–107	104–119
9"					92–98	98–100	106–122
10"					94–101	101–113	109–125
11"	106–114	112–113	120–135		96–104	104–116	112–128
5' 0"	109–117	115–126	123–138			107–119	115–131
1"	112–120	118–129	126–141		102–110	110–122	118–134
2"	115–124	121–133	129–144		105–113	110–122	118–134
3"	118–126	124–136	132–148		108–113	113–126	121–138
4"	121–129	127–139	135–152		111–119	120–135	129–146
5"	124–133	130–143	138–156		114–123	124–139	133–150
6"	128–137	134–147	142–161		122–131	128–143	137–154
7"	132–141	138–152	147–166		126–135	132–147	141–158
8"	136–145	142–156	151–170		130–140	136–151	145–163
9"	140–150	146–160	155–174		134–144	140–155	149–168
10"	144–154	150–165	159–179		138–148	144–159	153–173
11"	148–158	154–170	164–184		142–152	148–163	157–178
6' 0"	152–162	158–175	168–189		146–156	152–167	161–183
1"	156–167	162–180	173–194				
2"	160–171	167–185	178–199				
3"	164–175	172–190	182–204				
4"	168–179	177–195	186–209				

Factors Affecting the Digestive Processes

Factors Affecting Digestive Secretions

Increased Flow of Acid and Enzyme Production	Decreased Flow of Acid and Enzyme Production
☺ Stimulation of Seasonings, Spices and Acid Foods	Large Amounts of Fat ☹
☺ Attractive, Appetizing, Well-liked Foods	Large Meals ☹
☺ State of Happiness and Contentment	Poor Mastication of Food ☹
	Worry, Anger, Fear, Pain ☹
☺ Pleasant Surroundings when Eating	Poor Appearance, Flavor or Taste of Foods ☹

Factors Affecting Intestinal Tone and Motility

Increased Tone and Motility	Decreased Tone and Motility
☺ Warm Foods	Cold Foods ☹
☺ Liquid and Soft Foods	Dry, Solid Foods ☹
☺ Fibrous Foods	Low Fiber Foods ☹
☺ High Carbohydrate, Low Fat Foods	High Fat Foods ☹
☺ Seasonings	Vitamin B Complex Deficiency ☹
	Sedentary Habits ☹
	Fatigue ☹
	Worry, Anger, Fear, Pain ☹

GENERAL EATING FACTORS

✓ Eat Only When Hungry

✓ Do Not Over Eat

✓ Do Not Eat When in Pain or
  Emotionally Upset

✓ Do Not Eat When Tired or
  Immediately After Hard Work

✓ Eat Foods at Room Temperature

✓ Eat a Meal to Fit the Type of
  Work You Do

✓ Eat Juicy Foods Prior to
  Concentrated Foods

✓ Eat Raw Foods before Cooked Foods

Food Combination Charts
Acid Food & Neutral Food Chart

FRUITS	VEGETABLES	NUTS	NEUTRAL
All preserved or jellied, canned; sugared, dried, sulphured, glazed fruits, raw with sugar, bananas, if green tip, cranberries, olives, pickled, green	Artichokes Asparagus Tips, (white) Brussels Sprouts Dried Beans (all) Garbanzos Lentil Rhubarb	All nuts, (more so if roasted) Peanuts Coconut, dried Peanut	Sugar, refined Oils, Olives, Corn, Cotton Seed, Soy, Sesame, Fats, Lard and other Greases
DAIRY	**CEREALS**	**MISCELLANEOUS**	
Butter, Cheese, all Cottage Cheese Cream: ice cream, ices custard Milk, (boiled, cooked or pasteurized, malted, dried, canned	All Flour Products Buckwheat Barley Breads, (all kinds) Cakes Corn, Cornmeal, Cornflakes, Starch and Hominy Crackers (all) Doughnuts Dumplings Grapenuts Macaroni / Spaghetti Noodles Pies and Pastry Rice Rye-Krisp	All Alcoholic Beverages Candy and Confectionery Cocoa and Chocolate Coca-Cola Condiments, (i.e. curry, pepper, salt, spices, etc. Dressings and thick sauces Drugs and Aspirins Eggs, (especially whites) Ginger, (preserved) jams and Jellies Flavorings Marmalades Mayonnaise Preservatives (benzoate, sulphur, vinegar, salt brine, smoke) Sago (starch) Soda water Tapioca (starch) Tobacco, juice, snuff, smoke Vinegar Lack of Sleep Overwork Worry	
FRESH FOODS			
All meat, fowl, and fish, Beef tea Fish, shellfish (all) Gelatin Gravies			

COMBINATION CHART

One food at a meal is the most ideal for the easier and best digestion.
Combinations of several foods at a meal should be in accordance with this chart.

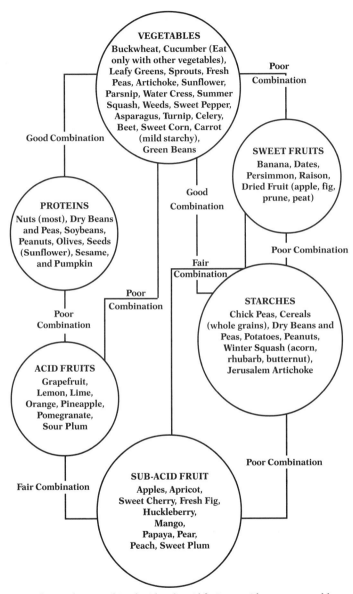

VEGETABLES
Buckwheat, Cucumber (Eat only with other vegetables), Leafy Greens, Sprouts, Fresh Peas, Artichoke, Sunflower, Parsnip, Water Cress, Summer Squash, Weeds, Sweet Pepper, Asparagus, Turnip, Celery, Beet, Sweet Corn, Carrot (mild starchy), Green Beans

SWEET FRUITS
Banana, Dates, Persimmon, Raison, Dried Fruit (apple, fig, prune, peat)

PROTEINS
Nuts (most), Dry Beans and Peas, Soybeans, Peanuts, Olives, Seeds (Sunflower), Sesame, and Pumpkin

STARCHES
Chick Peas, Cereals (whole grains), Dry Beans and Peas, Potatoes, Peanuts, Winter Squash (acorn, rhubarb, butternut), Jerusalem Artichoke

ACID FRUITS
Grapefruit, Lemon, Lime, Orange, Pineapple, Pomegranate, Sour Plum

SUB-ACID FRUIT
Apples, Apricot, Sweet Cherry, Fresh Fig, Huckleberry, Mango, Papaya, Pear, Peach, Sweet Plum

Poor Combination

Good Combination

Good Combination

Fair Combination

Poor Combination

Poor Combination

Poor Combination

Poor Combination

Poor Combination

Fair Combination

Avocados are best combined with sub-acid fruits or with green vegetables.
Melons (all kinds) should be eaten alone.

Bad Combinations	**Poor Combinations**	**Good Combinations**
Protein Starch	Protein and Acid Fruit	Protein and Leafy Greens
Oil and Starch	Leafy Greens and Acid Fruits	Starch and Vegetables
Fruit and Starch	Leafy Greens and Sub-Acid Fruits	Oil and Leafy Greens
		Oil and Acid, Sub-Acid Fruits

1) One food per meal for best digestion.

2) Do not mix more than four foods or food from more than two classifications.

3) Serve one protein food or one starch food per meal.

4) Oils slows digestion. Combines best with fruit, vegetables; combines poorly with starch, protein.

5) Tomato combines best with avocado, green vegetables.

6) Wheatgrass: Take on an empty stomach. May mix juice with carrot, green vegetable juice.

7) Seed yogurt: Goes well with ripe sub-acid fruit, leafy greens, sprouts, alone.

8) Honey or molasses: Best avoid, however eat alone on an empty stomach to prevent fermentation.

9) Peanuts are high in protein, starch, fat; they are also difficult to digest.

10) Dairy products: Best avoid—eat alone.

11) Fruit: Try eating one type at a time or combine them according to type of seed. Stone fruit (peach, nectarine, apricot, cherry), citrus fruit (apples, pear), dried fruit, melon fruit. Papaya goes well with all sub-acid fruit, as well a with banana.

ALKALINE FOOD CHART

FRUITS	VEGETABLES	VEGETABLES	MISCELLANEOUS
Apples and Cider	VEGE-BROTH	Potatoes	Agar
Apricots	Artichokes	Pumpkin	Alfalfa Products
Avocados	Asparagus, (ripe)	Radish	Coffee Substi-
Bananas, (speckled	Bamboo Shoots	Rhubarb (oxalic acid)	tutes
only)	Beans, (green, lima,	Rutabaga (swede)	Ginger Dries,
Berries (all)	string, sprouts)	Salsify	unsweetened
Breadfruit	Beets and Tops	Sauerkraut (lemon	Honey
Cactus	Broccoli	only)	Kelp (edible)
Cantaloupe	Cabbage, red and	Sorrel	Teas, unsweet-
Carob, (pod only)	white)	SOY BEANS	ened — all;
Cherimoyas	Carrots	Soy Bean Extract	desert and mate,
CRANBERRIES	Celery	Spinach	alfalfa, clover,
Cherries	Cauliflower	Squash	mint,
Citron	Chard	Taro, (baked)	oat oriental,
Currants	Chayotes	Turnips and Tops	sage,
Dates	Chicory	Water Chestnut	strawberry
Figs	Chives	Watercress	Yeast Cakes
Grapes	Collards		
Grapefruit	Cowslip	**DAIRY PRODUCTS**	**NUTS**
Guavas	Cucumber		
Kumquats	Dandelion Greens	Acidophilus	Almonds
Lemons, (ripe)	Dill	Buttermilk	Chestnuts
Limes	Dulse (sea Lettuce)	Koumiss	(roasted)
Loquat	Eggplant	Milk, (raw, human,	Coconut (fresh)
Mangoes	Endive	cow, or goat	
Melons, (all)	Escarole	Whey	
Nectarines	Garlic	Yogurt	
Olives (sundries)	Green Dock		
Papayas	Horseradish (fresh)	**FLESH FOODS**	
Passion Fruit	Jerusalem Artichoke		
Peaches	Kale	None, (blood and	
Pears	Kohlrabi	bones only are alkaline	
Persimmons	Leek	forming)	
Pineapple, (fresh	Legumes, (except		
if ripe)	peanut & Lentil)	**CEREALS**	
PLUMS	Lettuce and		
Pomegranates	Romaine	Corn, green (1st 24	
Pomelos	MUSHROOMS	hours)	
PRUNES and JUICE	(most varieties)		
Quince	Okra		
Raisins	Onions		
Sapotes	Oyster Plant		
Tamarind	Parsley		
Tangerines	Parsnips		
Tomatoes	Peppers, (green or		
	red)		

HEALTHFUL TIPS

HEALTHFUL TIPS

1. I feel the best exercises are walking, swimming, jumping rope, deep breathing: stretching, and cycling.

2. In my opinion, I believe women should wear low heal shoes, instead of high heel shoes. Jeans should not be worn tight, but loosely.

3. Men should wear boxer underwear, instead of jockey underwear; there should be room around the genital area for the testes to move freely.

4. Women should not use tampons, but Kotex (Mini, Maxi Thins). Tampons do not allow the menstrual toxins to be eliminated properly.

5. Women should wear cotton crotched underwear or all cotton underwear.

6. Women should douche only after their menstruation, but daily clean the vagina with natural soap and water.

7. For those who smoke cigarettes, Vitamin C and Vitamin A are destroyed in the body. Therefore, these two vitamins should be taken in supplements: Vitamin C—time released 6,000 mg. a day, Vitamin A—at least 25,000 I.U.'s a day.

8. For those women that suffer from miscarriages, Vitamin E is needed during the pregnancy—600 I.U.'s a day, and 400 mcg. a day of Folic Acid.

9. Water should be drank cool and not cold, warm and not hot.

10. Borax is a good fungus cleaner.

11. White vinegar is an excellent cleaner for windows and glass.

12. Use only white colored toilet paper, instead of colored toilet paper, due to the dyes in colored toilet paper.

13. Keep oil based vitamin and mineral supplements in the refrigerator.

WHEN SHOULD YOU EAT A MEAL?

The time that you eat is important for the body's metabolic reaction. There are two general classifications of normal chemical reactions in the body:

1) Anabolic, which are constructive and "buildup"

2) Catabolic, which are degradable and break substances down so they can be either utilized or eliminated.

TIPS FOR BETTER EATING HABITS

Eat between the hours of 6:00 a.m. and 4:00 p.m. Do not snack between meals; allow the food to digest properly—at least 6–10 hours, before you eat again

After you eat your meal you should wait at least 45 minutes to 1 hour before you drink something.

DO NOT EAT AND DRINK AT THE SAME TIME !!!

Whenever the seasons change, at the beginning you should always take a laxative, especially when the seasons change from winter to spring, (72 Hour Fast) Fruit Juices only. (Spring Equinox)

Every morning, first thing after you rise, drink warm water with a fresh squeezed lemon (½ lemon to a cup).

DO NOT DRINK SODAS—Only drink spring water and unsweetened fruit juices.

No iron supplements should be taken for they have a tendency to irritate the stomach and intestinal functions.

Liquid iron supplements are better than pill or capsule form.

ALL MEN should take Ginseng, Bee Pollen, Bee Propolis, Cayenne, Gotu-Kola, and Fo-Ti Daily, for stamina, vigor and endurance.

ALL WOMEN should take Dong-Quai, Royal Jelly, Bee Pollen, Bee Propolis daily for stamina, vigor, and endurance. Also for chronic cramps and female disorders before and after menstruation, especially Dong-Quai.

FOODS:

Dairy products should be taken in moderation, skim-milk, low-fat milk are better than whole-milk, due to the fat content. Cheese, ice-creams, sour creams, etc., should also be eaten in moderation, or not at all. (Lacto Vegetarians)

Additionally, eggs should be eaten in moderation and the yoke should only be eaten. The ironic part of this is that the yoke contains cholesterol and lecithin, which is the adversary of cholesterol. Eggs contain Salmonella today, and a lot of companies are not informing the public of this deadly bacteria. (Ovo-Vegetarians)

Eggs are also high in Albumen and Cholesterol. Eggs should not be eaten fried, poached, boiled, as omelettes, and so forth. Eggs should only be used in the baking of veggie roast and cakes when needed as a binder.

For Vegan Vegetarians, I recommend using Arrowroot, along with liquid lecithin as a binder for cooking.

Oils for Cooking and Salad (cold pressed)

* Extra Virgin Cold Pressed Olive Oil—Best

* Canola Oil

* Safflower Oil

Ginseng should be taken <u>every other</u> day, for people with HYPERTENSION it should be taken in moderation.

WATER

WHY EVERYBODY NEEDS APPROXIMATELY EIGHT CUPS OF WATER A DAY

"In health and sickness, pure water is one of heaven's choicest blessings. Its proper use promotes health. It is the beverage which god provided to quench the thirst of animals and man. Drunk freely, it helps to supply the necessities of the system and assists nature to resist disease."

Ellen G. White
The Ministry of Healing, P. 237

People may have heard that everyone should drink eight cups of water a day, but does everyone know why?

The answer is to maintain the body's proper water balance. Water is essential to life; it is present is all living body cells. If the body is to function properly, the body's daily output of water must be replenished. And research has shown that, for adults, approximately eight cups of water are needed to maintain the healthful water balance.

Even a physically inactive adult uses up eight cups of water daily, because water is the medium for virtually all the body's chemistry, and it is used constantly.

<u>Water is basic to balanced nutrition</u>—through perspiration. Perspiration occurs to some degree even when one is not aware of it; each day the skin of even a sedentary person loses moisture equal to two cups of water.

<u>Water is a lubricant</u>—preventing friction between the body's joints and muscles, the same way oil prevents friction between machinery parts. During manual labor and many strenuous sports, the body is stretched, twisted, and bent in ways that wouldn't be possible if water weren't present.

<u>Water intake minimizes dehydration</u>—for sweating that can result from long periods of exercise.

<u>Water reduces stress on the circulatory system</u>—during sports activities, and it helps the blood carry energy-providing carbohydrates to the body's cells.

<u>During illness, greater water intake helps regulate body temperature</u>—and control fever.

By using water for all its functions and losing water through perspiration and breathing, the body uses an average of three quarts each day. Most people consume approximately one quart in their daily diet, so where does the rest come from" In its simplest form, by drinking eight cups of water.

<u>The key to adequate water intake</u>: The urine should be pale. Water should be <u>drunken Cool</u> and not Cold, <u>Warm</u> and not Hot.

Water

Drink 6–8 oz. glasses of the following recommended spring waters each day.

- Evian Spring Water
- Mountain Valley Spring Water
- Poland Springs Spring Water

Distilled water will eliminated vitamins and minerals from the body.

There are harmful chemicals in tap drinking water, such as Chlorine, Aluminum, Sodium Fluoride, dissolved pipe metals (Iron, Zinc, etc.) Sodium Fluoride is used in rat poison, it is also found in Tap drinking water. Sodium Fluoride inhibits cell respiration, and since cancer cells are cells with lowered Oxidative capacity.

SALT
The average person in America consumes 30–50 pounds or more of salt each year. One should not exceed 500 milligrams a day of salt. Low sodium intake is the key to good health.

The following can be used in place of table salt:

1. Bragg's Liquid Aminos
2. Dr. Bronner's Liquid Boullion
3. <u>Fresh</u> Lemon or Lime Juice

FRUITS AND VEGETABLES

SOME VEGETABLES AND FRUITS TO BEWARE OF...

BEETS: (including beet greens) have high concentration of oxalic acid which can cause severe illness or death. The oxalic acid combines with calcium, forming insoluble calcium oxalate which settle in the bladder, kidneys and vital organs.

CRANBERRIES, PLUMS, AND PRUNES:
                Acid forming and decalcifying due to the presence of benzoic acid which is transformed into hippuric acid in the body.

ICEBERG LETTUCE:
                Contains lactucarium (a narcotic alkaloid bearing the resemblance to opium), which is present chiefly in the inner yellowish part of a head of lettuce, and in smaller amounts or Romaine Lettuce and green-colored leaf lettuce.

MUSHROOMS:
                Contain a high uric acid content.

OXALIC ACID:
                Is a compound found in spinach and other fruits and vegetables—the body cannot metabolize oxalic acid. Oxalic acid robs the body of calcium.

PEPPERS: Contain even more oxalic acid than spinach (see below). It is abutting to rhubarb in its high oxalic acid content.

BENZOIC ACID:
                A preservative that occurs in nature in cherry bark, Raspberries, Tea, Anise, and Cassia bark. First described in 1608 when it was found in gum benzoin. Mild irritant to skin, eyes, and mucous membranes, and reported to cause allergic reactions.

In understanding food chemistry, one must understand the difference of acid forming foods, and alkaline base forming foods.

Acid Forming Foods:

Thicken the blood and put a strain on the arteries and heart. Most grains are acid forming, except Millet and Buckwheat, which are considered to be alkaline. Sprouted seeds and grain become more alkaline in the process of sprouting.

Citric Acid:

Is metabolized in the body to become an alkaline ash. Since citric acid is metabolized in the body to alkaline ash, taking it away from someone who has an acid condition would be taking away the very thing which would help to get rid of the acid condition.

Acetic Acid:

Is found in Vinegar, which is metabolized in the body, but it has a deleterious effect on the liver, as does alcohol. It thickens the blood and puts a strain on the arteries and the heart. Vinegar also interferes with the digestion of starch. Vinegar lessens the alkaline reserve of the blood and tends to produce acidosis.

Tannic Acid:

Is found in Tea, Coffee, and Cocoa, for it is a drug. Tannic acid affects the mucous membranes of the digestive tract and especially the stomach and should not be used.

Oxalic Acid:

In order for the body to get rid of oxalic acid, it calls for a reserve of calcium. If there is not reserve, the body will take it from the bones and teeth because oxalic acid must unite with calcium to form tiny, minute crystals called cilium oxalate.

Phytic Acid:

Found in the bran of grains and the outer coating of legumes. Phytic Acid can tie up minerals like calcium, iron and zinc, thereby preventing their absorption.

Theobromine:

Is found in cocoa and chocolate, it also robs the body of calcium, and contributes to the cause of hypoglycemia. When Theobromine is absorbed into the blood stream from the stomach, the adrenal cortex glands which sits on top of the kidneys are stimulated by the Theobromine to secrete their hormone cortisone into the blood stream. When this hormone enters the blood stream it stimulates the liver, which changes its stored glycogen into glucose which it pours into the blood stream.

Calcium:

Is needed in metabolizing protein, for when there is not enough calcium in the diet, the body will take if from the bones and teeth, in order to properly metabolize the protein.

FOODS TO AVOID OR PREPARE WITH CALCIUM FOOD PRODUCTS, DUE TO THEIR OXALIC ACID CONTENT.

Beet Greens	Rhubarb Stems
Black Pepper	Sorrel
Cocoa	Spinach
Lamb's Quarters	Swiss Chard
Purslane Leaves	Tea (steeped 5 minutes)
Pokeweed	

FREE RADICALS
AND
OPPONENTS

FREE RADICALS

One of the dangers of radiation is that it encourages the formation of free radicals. A free radical is an atom or group that has at least on unpaired electron. Because another element can easily pick up this free electron and cause a chemical reaction, these free radicals can effect dramatic changes in the body. Hydrogen peroxide is an example of an unstable substance involved in free radical reactions. Because these free radicals are highly volatile, they can cause a lot of damage.

Free radicals are normally present in the body in small numbers. Biochemical processes naturally lead to the formation of free radicals, and under normal circumstances the body can keep them in check; however, exposing the body to ionizing radiation activates the formation of free radicals. The formation of a large number of free radicals stimulates to formation of more free radicals, leading to greater instability.

Damage is incurred due to excessive radical formation. The presence of a dangerous number of free radicals can alter the way in which the cells code genetic material. Changes in protein structure can occur as a result of errors in protein synthesis. The body's immune system may then see this altered protein as a foreign substance and try to destroy it. The formation of mutated proteins can eventually damage the immune system and lead to leukemia and cancer., as well as a host of other diseases.

In addition to damaging genetic material, free radicals can destroy the protective layer of fat in the cell membrane. The formation of free radicals can also lead to retention of fluid in the cells, which is involved in the aging process. Calcium levels in the body may be upset as well.

In addition to radiation, the diet can also contribute to the formation of free radicals. When the body obtains nutrients through the diet, it utilizes oxygen and these nutrients to create energy. In this oxidation process, oxygen molecules containing unpaired electrons are released. These oxygen free radicals can cause damage to the body in produced in extremely large amounts. A diet that is high in fat can increase free radical activity. Oxidation occurs more readily in fat molecules than it does in carbohydrate or protein molecules. Cooking fats in high temperatures, particularly frying foods in oil, can produce high numbers of free radicals. Supplementing the diet with antioxidants such as the enzymes superoxide dismutase and glutathione peroxidase, vitamins A, C, and E and the trace mineral selenium and germanium can inhibit the formation of these free radicals by pairing up the free electrons. By preventing free radical formation, antioxidants help to detoxify the body.

FOODS USED TO COMBAT FREE RADICALS IN THE BODY (HERBS AND VITAMINS)

1. Astragalus
2. Pycnogenol
3. Vitamin C (time release, buffered) 6,000 milligrams daily
4. Vitamin E 400—I.U. daily
5. Echinacea Root Capsule or Tablet—to be taken every other day
6. Beta-Carotene Vitamin A—25,000 I.U.s daily
7. Kyolic Garlic capsules—to be taken every day
8. Bee Propolis
9. Suma
10. Microhydrin—take one capsule three times a day

FREE RADICALS:

A free radical is an atom or group of atoms that has at least one unpaired electron. Because another element can easily pick up this free electron and cause a chemical reaction, these free radicals can effect dramatic and destructive changes in the body. Free radicals are activated in heated and rancid oils and by radiation in the atmosphere—among other things.

FREE RADICAL SCAVENGER:

A substance that removes or destroys free radicals.

Alkaline forming foods are better for vibrant health as opposed to acid forming foods.

Our diets should consist of 80% Alkaline foods and 20% acid foods —our stomachs are Alkaline

<u>Unfiltered</u>

| Digestive Enzymes | [Bromelin—Pineapple] [Pectin—Apple Juice] [Papain—Papaya Juice] | Digestive Enzymes Juices |

It is very important to drink the above-mentioned juices on a daily basis.

Enzymes are the catalyst for life. Eat RAW fruits and RAW vegetables daily. When the enzymes are destroyed in the food we ingest they cause free radicals in the body.

Citric Acid is metabolized in the body to become an Alkaline Ash.

Food enzymes are designed to reintroduce to the diet the vital enzymes missing from most modern diets, especially <u>plant enzymes.</u>

1. Protease—for protein

2. Amylase & Cellulase—for carbohydrates and dietary fiber

3. Lipase—for fat

BREAD

BREAD...
CHEMICAL FERTILIZERS, SEED PRESERVATIVES AND SPRAYS

The chemical poisoning of bread starts on the farm. If the grain from which the bread is made is grown on land contaminated by past chemical fertilizer and insecticide (as well as weed-killer) residues, resulting from application to previous crops (and what American farmlands were not thus cumulatively contaminated?), these chemicals will be taken up by growing plants and will find their way to the wheat or rye that is harvested from the crop, even if no further chemicals were used. But, as a matter of fact, chemicals are used on all grain crops, which are raised with chemical fertilizers and insecticides (i.e., DDT, etc.). That is why so many people are buying organically grown grains and flours directly from organic farmers who do not use chemical fertilizers, sprays of fumigants.

A source of chemical contamination of grain are the chemical seed preservatives with which the seed is treated before planting in order to free it from disease carrying smut and rust organisms. There is reason to believe that the poison thus applied to seeds definitely penetrates into them and that some of it will show up in the seed of the new crop used to make flour. Practically all wheat seed has been treated with a mercury containing poison named "Cerium." (It is claimed that potato seed is also treated with a mercury containing compound to prevent rotting of cut potatoes after planting.) Wheat seed treated with it is so poisonous that bags in which it is packed are marked "caution," with instructions not to feed it to farm animals.

WHEAT IS URIC ACID FORMING

Though wheat has always been considered to be "the staff of life," and has been a basic carbohydrate in the diet of Occidental races since ancient times, a greater part of the world's two billion inhabitants, living in Asia, Africa, and Latin America, used rice or millet in place of wheat. Wheat is an acid binder, and the aforementioned grains, such as rice and millet should be consumed instead of wheat. Rice is low in uric Acid, however, millet is completely alkaline.

CHEESE

Chapter on Cheese

During the fermentation or curing of cheese a mixed group of microorganisms grows in the milk curd. Protein, fat, and carbohydrates are the major nutrients affected during the curing process. The protein portion of cheese is fermented to peptide amines, indols, skatol, and ammonia. The fat in cheese is hydrolyzed to irritating fatty acids, butyric, caproic, caprylic, and longer carbon chain fatty acids. The carbohydrate of milk, mainly lactose, is converted to lactic acid by putrefaction. Most of the products of fermentation are toxic and irritating, including the esters, the acids, and certain of the amines, including tyramine and nitrosamine.

A summary of the objectionable features of hard or ripened cheeses includes the following:

1. The putrefactive process results in the production of amines, ammonia, irritation fatty acids (butyric, caroic, caprylic, etc.). The carbohydrate is converted to lactic acid. These are all waste products which cause irritation to nerves and gastrointestinal tract.

2. Migraine headaches can be caused by tyramine, one of the toxic amines produced in cheese.

3. Certain of the amines can interact with the nitrates present in the stomach to form nitrosamine, a cancer producing agent.

4. An intolerance to lactose, the chief carbohydrate of cheese and milk, is probably the most common food sensitivity in America.

5. Rennet is used in the curdling of milk for cheese making. Rennet is obtained from the whole stomach lining of calves, lambs, kids, or pigs.

Our counsel has been a great blessing to us for many years. Think how much suffering has been avoided because we have had the counsel on cheese. "Cheese should never be introduced into the stomach." (1) "Children are allowed to eat flesh meats, spices, butter, cheese, pork, rich pastries, and condiments generally. These things do their work of deranging the stomach, exciting the nerves to a natural action and enfeebling the intellect." (2)

"If milk is used, it should be thoroughly sterilized; with this precaution there is less danger of contracting disease from its use. Butter is less harmful when eaten on cold bread than when used in cooking; but, as a rule, it is better to dispense with it altogether. Cheese is still more objectionable; it is wholly unfit for food." (3) "Some brought cheese to the meeting, and ate it; although new, it was altogether too strong for the stomach, and should never be introduced into it. (4) Pasteurization of milk does not "thoroughly" sterilize it. To be "thoroughly sterilized," milk should be boiled about 20 minutes. Pasteurization only elevates the temperature of the milk for a few seconds, and that not even to the boiling point.

Since cheese and cream cheese are not "ripened" it would seem reasonable that these products could be used. They are safe, however, only if free from disease producing organisms, heavy metals, detergents, antibiotics, cancer viruses, and other undesirable substances. In this day of expanding diseases in animals, and expanding processes of manufacture and marketing, it is unlikely that any dairy products can be considered safe. "Animals from which milk is obtained are not always healthy. They may be diseased. A cow may be apparently well in the morning, and die before night. Then she was diseased in the morning, and her milk was diseased, but you did not know it. The animal is diseased." (5)

"The light given me is that it will be very long before we shall have to give up animal food. Even milk will have to be discarded. Disease is accumulating rapidly. " (6)

(1) Ellen G. White, <u>Counsels on Diet and Foods</u>, P. 368

(2) White, <u>Volume 3 of the Testimonies</u>, P. 136

(3) White, <u>The Ministry of Healing</u>, P. 302

(4) White, <u>Review & Herald</u>, July 19, 1980

(5) White, <u>Counsels on Diet& Foods</u>, P. 356–357

(6) White, <u>Counsels on Diet & Foods</u>, P. 357

SUGAR

REFINED SUGAR

A. Steals calcium from the body

B. To Refine Sugar, sixty four food ingredients are eliminated.

    I. Potassium, magnesium, calcium, iron, manganese, phosphate, and sulfate are among the discarded minerals.

    II. A, D, and the B-Complex, essential enzymes, amino acids, fibers and unsaturated fats are all removed.

    III. Most of the B-Complex vitamins are absorbed into a by-product known as blackstrap molasses (crude).

CONVERTED SUGAR

    I. Glucose by the digestive juices

    II. Carried through the bloodstream to the pancreas—which produces insulin

    III. Eating excessive amounts of sugar over stimulates the pancreas into producing a excess of insulin.

    IV. Diabetes results from an inadequate supply of insulin and too much sugar in the blood.

    V. Exhausted from the constant demand of producing insulin to convert all that sugar into heat and energy, the pancreas will finally malfunction and the excess sugar then pollutes the bloodstream.

SUGAR NOTES

The average American consumes about 2½ lbs. a day of sugar.

Adding sugar to boxed products gives it weight and increases the shelf life.

One-in-five Americans wear false teeth by the age of 50.

Sugar feeds the bacteria normally present in the mouth and causes them to multiply. These bacteria adhere to the surfaces of the teeth, forming a deposit known as plaque.

Tooth enamel is the strongest material in the body, however, the bacteria inside the plaque is able to eat through it and attack the dentine in side.

THE AVERAGE AFRICAN AMERICAN CONSUMES 50–100 lbs. OF REFINED SUGAR ANNUALLY

The following can be used in place of sugar:

1. Date Sugar
2. Brown Rice Syrup
3. Tueplo Honey
4. Stevia

MINERALS

CALCIUM:

Need:
>
> Contributes to formation of strong bones and teeth. Helps clot blood, regulates heart, and maintain mineral balance in the body.
>
> Calcium, Phosphorus and Vitamin D help prevent softening of bones which occurs in Rickets. Vitamin D must be present for proper calcium utilization.

Sources of Calcium:
>
> Alfalfa, almonds, arrowroot, cabbage (savoy) cauliflower, green leafy vegetables, (broccoli, collard, dried beans and figs, kale, mustard, turnip), millet, molasses (Blackstrap), oranges, pineapple, soybeans, sprouts, tofu (soybean cheese) whole grains.

Deficiency of Calcium in the Body:
>
> Brittle bones, dental cavities, excessive bleeding, rickets, poor bone development.
>
> Calcium is very important for women, because the lack of calcium can cause Osteoporosis (the gradual loss of bone mass resulting in increased fractures) the bones become soft. This condition is prevalent mostly in <u>white</u> women. A person needs 1,000 mg. a day of calcium for if the <u>body</u> does not receive the adequate amount of calcium, then the body will take the calcium from the bones, teeth and muscle.

IODINE:

Need:
>
> Essential to thyroid gland in making a hormone which regulates the rate of food that is burned in the body. This hormone is important for proper growth and development. Deficiency of iodine causes simple goiter;

and enlargement of the thyroid gland. This condition is prevalent around the Great Lakes and Pacific Northwest Regions.

Sources of Iodine:
>
> Dulse, green leafy vegetables that is grown near the seashore or in soil that is not depleted of iodine content, kelp, kombu, nori, wakambe.

Deficiency of Iodine in the Body:
>
> Simple goiter, retarded physical, sexual and mental development in young people. Deficiency can also cause weight gain and metabolism disorder, such as your endocrine system.

IRON:

> Total amount of iron found in the body is less than the weight of one-cent piece. About 3 grams in actual weight or .004% of body composition.

Need:
>
> Small amount of iron in all body cells. Most iron is Red blood cells helps to form hemoglobin, red coloring matter of red blood cells, which is vital to transporting oxygen to every body cell. Insufficient iron in diet causes anemia.

Sources of Iron
>
> Almonds, beets, breads, dried beans, dried fruits (apricots, peaches, prunes), grain cereals, green leafy vegetables, (chard, kale, turnip tops). Blackstrap Molasses, oatmeal, peas (dried, split), plantain, raisins, spirulina, sprouts, soybean, wheat grass, whole grain cereals.

Deficiency of Iron in the Body:
>
> Causes anemia, pale complexion, lowered vitality, retarded development, decreased red blood cells and

hemoglobin. Iron is very important for women, due to the menstrual cycle and menstrual irregularity (lack of iron).

MAGNESIUM: (nerve, digestive, laxative)

Promotes new cells, relaxes nerves, prevents and relieves constipation, activates enzymes.

Sources of Magnesium:
Barley, coconut, eggplant, figs, grapefruit, oranges, spirulina, whole grains.

Good for those who suffer from hypertension (High Blood Pressure and Insomnia)

MANGANESE: (hemoglobin—enzyme activator)

Aids in forming hemoglobin, activates enzymes, improves memory.

Sources of Manganese:
Bananas, blueberries, bran, beans, beets, chard, grains, leafy greens, peas. Good for those who suffer from Diabetes, and Pancreas disorders.

PHOSPHORUS:

Calcium and phosphorus comprise 95% of minerals found in bones. Twice as much calcium and phosphorus in body as all other minerals combined.

Need:
Phosphorus is found in the nucleus of each cell. Combined with calcium, phosphorous helps form and maintain bones and teeth. It assists body cells to absorb food and get rid of wastes. Abundant in nervous tissue

(brain and nerve cells) found in blood stream and muscle tissue, essential to normal glandular system. Vitamin D is important in absorption of phosphorus.

Sources of Phosphorus:
Barley, Bran, dried beans, kelp, soyalecithin, lentils, millet, oatmeal, peanuts, rye, soybeans, spirulina, whole grain.

Deficiency of Phosphorus in the Body:
Perverted appetite, retarded growth, loss of weight, weakness, imperfect bone and teeth development. Good for those who suffer from Osteoporosis—balanced with Calcium.

POTASSIUM: (Cells and tissues secretion mineral)

Regular use of acid base balance, maintains weight, muscle toner. Good for nerves, good disposition, grace, beauty.

Sources of Potassium:
Bananas, Almonds, beans, blueberries, cabbage, coconut, dried fruits, dandelion, fresh vegetables, molasses, nuts, oats, olives, parsley, peaches, potato skins, spirulina, sprouts, watercress, whole grains. Good for those who suffer from Hypertension (High Blood Pressure) especially those of African origin.

SILICON: (Silica) Skeleton structure: bones, teeth, hair, skin, nails.

Eyes, keen hearing, tones up body, and infection resistance, silicon counteracts the effects of Aluminum in the body and it is important in the prevention of Alzheimer's disease and Osteoporosis.

Sources of Silicon:
Asparagus, barley, cabbage, cucumbers, flax, horse-

tail, oats, seeds, spinach, strawberries, tomatoes. Good for those who suffer from Eczema.

SODIUM: (maintains body fluids)

Normal heart action, body equilibrium, preserves balance between calcium and potassium, regulates body fluids, aids digestion.

Sources of Sodium:
Asparagus, beets, carrot, celery, coconut, cucumber, figs, oatmeal, okra, string beans, turnips.

SULPHUR: (brain and body tissues)

Relieves dermatitis and Eczema, iron balance of tissues, synthesis of body proteins, healthy hair and nails.

Sources of Sulphur:
Almonds, asparagus, avocados, bell peppers, broccoli, cabbage, cauliflower, chestnuts, eggplant, lentils, mustard greens, nuts, onions, other legumes, soybeans, whole grains.

ZINC:

Helps normal tissue function, protein and carbohydrates metabolism. Good for prostrate glands.

Sources of Zinc:
Alfalfa, bee pollen, pumpkin seeds, spirulina, wheat germ. Good for those who suffer from Diabetes.

COPPER:

Aids in the formation of Red Blood cells, part of many enzymes converts Amino Acid to hair pigment, also works with Vitamin C to form Elastin.

Sources of copper:
Nuts, dried legumes.

CHLORINE: (digestive system)

A body cleanser—eliminate wastes.

Sources of Chlorine:
Coconut, beets, radishes, sea salt, goat's milk.

SELENIUM:

As an antioxidant, selenium protects the immune system by preventing the formation of free radicals. Selenium and Vitamin E act synergistically to aid in the reproduction of antibodies, and help to maintain a healthy heart.

FLUORINE: (bones and teeth)

Disease register, knits bones, body beautifier.

Sources of Fluorine:
Cabbage, cauliflower, sprouts, watercress, spinach, tomatoes, brussels sprouts.

MOLYBDENUM

This essential is needed in extremely small amounts for nitrogen metabolism, which enables the body to use nitrogen. It aids in the final stages of conversion of purines to Uric acid. It also promotes normal cell function, and is part of the enzyme system of xanthine oxidase. A deficiency may cause sexual impotence in older males. Sources of Molybdenum Legumes, cereal grains, peas, and dark leafy green vegetables.

VITAMINS
VITAMINS
VITAMINS
VITAMINS
VITAMINS
VITAMINS

VITAMINS

VITAMIN A:

Builds resistance to infections, especially of the respiratory tract. Helps maintain a healthy condition of the outer layers of many tissues and organs. Promotes growth and vitality, formation of visual purple in the eye, counteracts night blindness and weak eyesight. Vitamin A promotes healthy skin. Essential for pregnancy and lactation.

Foods that Contain Vitamin A:
Apricots, asparagus, avocado, bee pollen cantaloupe, carob, carrots, celery, chicory, dandelion, endive, kale, lettuce, oranges, parsley, prunes, pumpkin, royal jelly, spinach, spirulina, tomatoes, turnip leaf, watercress.

Good for those who suffer from any form of cancer, and those who suffer from dry skin. Smokers (see Helpful Hints Page)

VITAMIN B_1:   (Thiamine)

Promotes growth, aids growth and digestion. This vitamin is essential for normal functioning of nerve tissues, muscles and heart.

Foods that Contain Vitamin B_1:
Almond, asparagus, avocado, bran, Brazil nuts, brown rice, cabbage, carob, carrots, celery, cashews, coconut, dandelion, grapefruit, grape juice, kelp powder, lemon, oatmeal, parsley,, peanuts, pineapple, pomegranate, pumpkin, radish, royal jelly, sunflower seeds, spirulina, turnip leaf, watercress, whole wheat.

Good for those who suffer from any brain disorder.

VITAMIN B$_2$: (Riboflavin)

Improves growth; essential for healthy eyes, skin and mouth. Promotes general good health. Good for those who suffer from Cataracts, B$_2$ will eliminate dandruff, also during pregnancy, the lack of this vitamin may damage the fetus. Cracks and sores at the corner of the mouth.

Foods that Contain Vitamin B$_2$:
Apple, apricot, broccoli, cabbage, carrots, chlorella, coconut, dandelion, dates, grapefruit, greens, kelp, mustard, prune, royal jelly, spinach, sunflower seeds, turnip leaf, watercress, wheat bran.

VITAMIN B$_3$: (Niacin) Niacinamide, Nicotinic Acid

Increases the utilization of carbohydrates and protein. Useful for the nervous system, skin, circulation, cold feet and hands, digestion. Good for those who suffer from heart irregularities—Niacin lowers cholesterol.

Foods that Contain Vitamin B$_3$:
Broccoli, carrots, corn flour, potatoes, tomatoes and whole wheat.

Vitamin B$_6$:   (Pyridoxine)

Aids in food assimilation and in protein and fat metabolism. Prevents various nerve and skin disorders; as well as nausea.

Foods that Contain Vitamin B$_6$:
Avocados, bananas, blackstrap molasses, brown rice, cabbage, cantaloupe, carrots, chlorella, corn, green leafy vegetables, green pepper, pecans, potatoes, royal jelly, yams, wheat germ, wheat grass.

Good for those who suffer from Asthma and arthritis, also those who suffer from water retention.

PABA: (Para-Aminobenzoic Acid) Vitamin B

A growth promoting factor, possibly in conjunction with Folic Acid, in experimental tests on animals. This vitamin, when omitted from foods cause hair to turn white. When restored to the diet, the white half turns black. This anti-oxidant helps protect against sunburn and skin cancer, acts as a coenzyme in the breakdown and utilization of protein.

Foods that Contain Paba:
Blackstrap molasses, brewers's yeast, whole grains.

PANTOTHENIC ACID: (Vitamin B_5)

Helps in the building of body cells and maintaining normal skin growth; the development of central nervous systems, required for synthesis of antibodies. Necessary for normal digestive processes. The anti-stress vitamin, it helps in the production of adrenal hormones and the formation of antibodies. It helps to produce vital steroids and cortisone in the adrenal gland, and is an essential element of coenzyme.

Foods that Contain Pantothenic Acid:
Broccoli, brown rice, cabbage, cauliflower, chick peas, filberts, kale, lentils, mushrooms, oatmeal, peas, sesame seeds, soybeans, sunflower seeds, walnuts, wheat bran.

Good for those who suffer from hair loss.

VITAMIN B_{12}:   (Cobalamin)

Helps in the formation and regeneration of red blood cells, thus helping to prevent anemia; a general tonic for adults. It also promotes growth and increased appetite in children. Good for those who suffer from infertility, and memory loss.

Foods that Contain Vitamin B_{12}:
    Beets, cauliflower, chlorella, grape juice (concord), kelp, royal jelly, sunflower seeds, wheat grass, whole wheat, Tofu (soybean cheese).

VITAMIN B_{13}:   (Orotic Acid)

Good for reproduction of cells.

Foods that Contain Vitamin B_{13}:
    Fermented Foods. Apple cider vinegar (Bragg's).

VITAMIN B_{15}: (Pangamic Acid)

Cell oxidation and respiration, metabolism (protein, fat and sugar). Also glandular and nervous system stimulation.

Foods that Contain Vitamin B_{15}:
    Apricot, bee pollen, brown rice, seeds (pumpkin, sesame, sunflower), kernel, whole grains.

BIOTIN: (Vitamin H)

Growth promoting factor, possibly related to metabolism of fats, and in the conversion of certain amino acids.

Foods that contain Biotin:
    Bananas, cauliflower, corn filberts, hazel nuts, lima beans, royal jelly, strawberries, wheat.

Good for those who suffer from hair loss.

VITAMIN C:

Necessary for healthy teeth, gums, and bones, strengthens all connective tissues, promotes wound healing, helps promote capillary integrity and prevention of permeability (a very important factor in maintaining sound health and vigor).

Foods that Contain Vitamin C:
Acerola, berries, broccoli leaf, cabbage, chard, cherries, citrus fruit, green leafy vegetables, guavas, honeydew melons, logan berries, paprika, peppers, persimmons, pineapple, radishes, red currants, rose hips, royal jelly, rutabagas, tomatoes.

NOTE: Vitamin C is easily destroyed by cooking.

Good for those who suffer from Oral and Genital Herpes, and bleeding gums. Smokers (see Helpful Hints Page)

INOSITOL:

Vital nutrient for blood cholesterol, overweight, mental problems, hair and heart. It also helps remove fats from the liver.

Foods that Contain Inositol:
Fruits, dark leafy vegetables and whole grains.

CHOLINE:

Regulate the functions of the liver. It is necessary for normal fat metabolism. It also minimizes excessive deposits of fats in liver. Also good for high blood pressure.

Good for those who suffer from memory loss.

Foods that Contain Choline:
Green leafy vegetables, legumes (soy beans), lecithin, wheat germ.

VITAMIN D: (Sunshine Vitamin)

Regulates the use of calcium and phosphorus in the body and is therefore necessary for the proper formation of teeth and bones. Vitamin D is very important in infancy and childhood.

Foods that Contain Vitamin D:
Alfalfa, bee pollen, chlorella, Natural sunshine, vegetable oils, wheat grass.

VITAMIN E:

Exact functions in humans are not yet known. Medical articles have been published on its value in helping to prevent sterility and as it pertains to the treatment of abortion aftercare. In muscular dystrophy—prevention of calcium deposits in blood vessel walls. Has been used favorably by some doctors in treatment of heart condition. Antioxidant that prevents cancer and Cardiovascular disease. Good for circulation, repairs tissue, and is useful in treating fibro cystic breasts and premenstrual syndrome. Vitamin E retards aging and may prevent age spots as well.

Vitamin E also prevents cell damage by inhibiting lipid peroxidation and the formation of free radicals.

Foods that Contain Vitamin E:
Green leafy vegetables, margarine (safflower, wheat germ oil, corn oil margarine), vegetable oil, wheat germ oil, whole grain cereals, whole wheat.

VITAMIN F:

A growth promoting factor, necessary for healthy skin, hair and glands, Promotes the availability of calcium to the cells. Now considered to be important in lowering blood cholesterol and in combating heart disease.

Foods that Contain Vitamin F:
Vegetables oils, e.g. corn, cottonseed, linseed, peanut, safflower, sesame seed and soybean.

FOLIC ACID: (Vitamin B)

Essential to the formation of red blood cells by its action on the bone marrow, it aids in protein metabolism and contributes to normal growth. It is also considered a brain food, and it is important for healthy cell division and replication. It may also help people who suffer from depression and anxiety and may be effective in the treatment of uterine cervical dysplasia. Folic acid works best when combined with Vitamin B_{12}.

Foods that Contain Folic Acid:
Almonds, apricots, asparagus, avocados, broccoli, brown rice, brussels sprouts, cabbage, cauliflower, coconuts, corn, dates, kale, all green leafy vegetables, lima beans, lentils, oats, peas, potato, royal jelly, squash, turnips, watercress, wheat, zucchini.

VITAMIN K:

Essential for the production of prothrombin (a substance which aids the blood in clotting). It is important for proper liver functions. Good for those who suffer from Osteoporosis. Vitamin K converts glucose into glycogen, for storage in the liver.

Foods that Contain Vitamin K:
Brussels sprouts, Blackstrap Molasses, Oatmeal, cauliflower, Alfalfa, chlorella, green leafy vegetables, soybean oil, sprouts, safflower oil.

VITAMIN P: Bioflavonoid—Citrus Flavonoid Compounds)

Strengthens walls of capillaries. Prevents Vitamin C from being destroyed in the body by oxidation. Beneficial in hypertension (high blood pressure). Reported to help resistance in infections and colds, Vitamin P have an ant bacterial effect and promote circulation, stimulate bile production. Good for those who suffer from oral herpes.

Foods that Contain Vitamin P:
Apricots, black currants, cherries, peels and pulp of citrus fruit, (especially lemons), parsley, plum, prune, rose hips and walnuts.

VITAMIN U: (antiulcer vitamin)

Foods that contain Vitamin U:
Cabbage, green vegetables, leaf, celery, raw greens.

RUTIN:

Goods for those who suffer from hypertension (high blood pressure)

Foods that Contain Rutin:
Buckwheat

VITAMIN B_{17}:   (Laetrile)

Has no know function in the human body, however, studies have shown its use in the treatment of cancer.

Foods that contain vitamin B_{17}:
Apricot kernel.

SUBSTANCES THAT ROB THE BODY OF NUTRIENTS

Different substances deplete the body of different nutrients. Use the list below to determine which supplements should be added to the diet when on prescription or over-the-counter medication. Some products like alcohol, caffeine, and fluoride are also listed. These rob the body of vitamins and minerals as well.

Substance	Depleted Nutrients
Alcohol	Magnesium, vitamin B Complex, vitamins C, D, E, and K
Allopurinol	Iron
Antacids	Calcium phosphate, vitamins A, B complex and D
Antibiotics	Vitamins B and K (Antibiotics also deplete the body of "friendly" bacteria.)
Antihistamines	Vitamin C
Aspirin	Calcium, folic acid, iron, potassium, vitamins A, B, complex, and C
Barbiturates	Vitamin C
Caffeine	Biotin, inositol, potassium, thiamine (vitamin B_1), zinc.
Carbamazepine	(Dilutes) blood sodium
Chlorothiazide	Magnesium, potassium
Cimetidine	Iron
Clonidine (alpha-adrenergic blocker)	Calcium, vitamin B complex
Corticosteroid	Calcium, vitamins A, B_6, and D, potassium, zinc
Digitalis preparations	Thiamine (B_1) vitamins B_6 (pyridoxine), zinc
Diphenyl-hydantoin (dilantin)	Vitamin D
Diuretics	Calcium, iodine, magnesium, potassium, riboflavin (B_2), vitamin C, zinc
Estrogen	Folic acid, vitamin B_6, (pyridoxine)
Fluoride	Vitamin C
Glutethimide	Folic acid, vitamin B_6

Guanethidine (and false neurotransmitter)	Magnesium, potassium, riboflavin (B_2), vitamin B_6 (pyridoxine)
Hydralazine	Vitamin B_6 (pyridoxine)
Indomethacin	Iron
Isoniazid	Niacin, vitamin B_6 (pyridoxine)
Laxatives (excluding herbs)	Potassium, vitamin B_6 (pyridoxine)
Lidocaine	Calcium, potassium
Nadolol	Choline, chromium, pantothenic acid (B_5)
Nitrates and Enitrites (coronary Vasodilators	Niacin, selenium, Pangamic acid (B_{15}), vitamins C, and
Oral contraceptives	Vitamin B complex, vitamins C, D, and E
Penicillin	Niacin (B_3) niacinamide, vitamin B_6 (pyridoxine)
Phenobarbital	Folic acid, vitamin B_6, (pyridoxine), vitamin B_{12}, vitamins D and K
Phenylbutazone	Folate, folic acid and iodine.
Phenytoin	Calcium, Folic Acid, Vitamin B_{12}, C, and K
Prednisone	Potassium, vitamin B_6 (pyridoxine) and C, zinc
Propranolol	Choline, chromium, pantothenic acid (B_5)
Quinidine	Choline, pantothenic acid (B_5), potassium, vitamin K
Reserpine (sympathetic inhibitor)	Phenylalanine, potassium, riboflavin (B_2), vitamin B_6 (Pyridoxine)
Spironolactone	Calcium, folic acid
Sulfa drugs	PABA (Sulfa drugs also destroy "friendly" bacteria)
Thiazides	Magnesium, potassium, riboflavin (B_{12}), zinc.
Triamterene	Calcium, folic acid
Trimethoprim	Folic acid

HERBS

HERBS FOR COOKING, BAKING & SALADS[10]

ANISE   (Pimpinella Anisum)

This is an annual herb, meaning it should be planted each year and is propagated from seeds. This growing height ranges from 1½ to 2 feet. It looks very similar to Dill. The growth maturation requirements for this plant are full sunlight with fairly dry soil.

Anise seeds are most commonly used in teas, baking cookies, and cakes. The leaves are often used in salads.

Sweet BASIL   (Ocimum Basilicum)

This is another annual herb which is propagated from its seeds. It grows from 2 to 3 feet in height. It is best grown in full sunlight and with mineral rich soil. The scent of Basil leaves is similar to that of Cloves.

Basil is widely used in all types of cooking dishes that contain tomatoes, beans: cheese, as well as in appetizers.

CARAWAY   (Carum Carvil)

A biennial herb with seeds that matures when two years old; around the middle of summer. Its height ranges from 1½ to 2 feet, and should be instilled in good soil, that is directly sighted by the full sun. The foliage of this herb is similar to carrot tops and produces white flowers. The seeds should be cut when they turn brown before they scatter.

Caraway seeds add zest and flavor to cooked vegetables such as cabbage, sauerkraut, carrots, potatoes, and onions, and soups. Also add to baked goods.

DILL   (Anethum Graveolens)

This is a natural herb which grows approximately 3 feet high. It should be planted in full sun and good soil. It produces yellow flowers when propagated each year.

Fresh dill leaves are especially tasty in cucumber salads, cottage cheese, coleslaw, vegetable salads, potatoes, peas, beans, tomatoes, and spinach. The whole plant, minus the roots are used in making pickles. Dill seeds are also used for vinegar, seeds cakes, and breads.

FENNEL   (Foeniculum Vulgares)

Propagated from seed, this perennial plant grows to a height of 5 feet. This herb should be grown in good soil with full sun. The heads are heavy with yellow flowers and should be staked or supported.

The stems of this herb can be used like celery. The seeds are used in teas and breads. The seeds and leaves add a licorice flavor to soups and pickles.

GARLIC   (Allium Sativum)

This plant grows to a height of 2 feet. It has pink flowers within small heads. It is a annual herbage that is propagated by separating the cloves and planted in spring. Like an onion, garlic is harvested in late summer or early fall when the leaves turn b grown. Garlic is stored like an onion.

There are many uses for garlic. It has often been called the "poor man's penicillin," because of its high medicinal value. The most common uses of garlic are cooking, salads, soups, sauces.

LEMON BALM   (Melissa Officinalis)

White flowers and a growth stature of 2 feet are characteristics of this herb. It should be planted in fairly moist soil and partly shaded lighting.

Lemon Balm is used fresh in beverages like mint. The dried leaves are widely used for tea and salads.

Sweet MARJORAM (Marjorana Hortensis)

Marjoram is actually a perennial but should be treated as an annual and planted fresh each year. It is propagated from seed very easily and grows to a height of 10 to 12 inches tall with white flowers. It thrives best in soil that is dry which receives direct sunlight.

Marjoram leaves are used in salad dressings, salads, vinegars, soups, and cooked vegetables.

MINT (Mentha Viridis)

This plant grows to a height of 12 inches with purple flowers. Mint is very easy to grow as a result of its cultivation in moist soil and partially shaded from the sun. When home grown, it is best grown in a container as it spreads very rapidly. This way it can be kept under better control.

Mint leaves can be used fresh or dry. Mint is very popular as a tea; when mixed with other herbs, such as Lemon Balm, or Alfalfa is makes for a delicious hot or cold tea. Additionally, mint is often used when making sauces. In salads, drinks or sprinkled on...fresh fruits, it adds a cool refreshing, aromatic flavor.

Herbal Remedies

This applies to all of herbal combinations
mentioned in this chapter:

A) Never boil leaves, flowers, herbs.
Steep them in water with the leafs or flowers removed from
the fire.
Steep about 10–15 minutes.

B) Roots and bark herbs should be boiled under low flame with
water for approximately 30 minutes to an hour.

ANTITOXINS

Chamomile
Echinacea
Elecampane
Golden Seal Root

ARTHRITIS

Alfalfa, Devil's Claw, Yucca Juice, Cherry
Juice Mistletoe, Add 1 teaspoon of each of
the above herbs to a gallon of water.

AFTER BIRTH

Balm
Feverfew
Shepherd's Purse

ATHLETE'S FOOT

Chamomile
Elecampane
Golden Seal Root
Tea Tree Oil

BLOOD PURIFIERS

Burdock
Cerosie
Dandelion
Gentian Root
Red Clover
Sassafras
Yellow Dock

BRAIN CELLS AND MEMORY

Cowslips
Ginkgo
Pimpernel
Foti
Gotu Kola

Blessed Thistle
Sage

BRONCHIAL & LUNG DISORDERS

Black Pine
Garlic
Hyssop
St. Johnswort
Coltsfoot
Horehound
Lungwort
Sundew
Vervain

CANCER

Blue Violet
Periwinkle
Red Clover
Chaparral
Rose Hips (5 10 grams per day)
Taheebo
Yellow Dock Root
Cat's Claw

CATARACTS

Cannabis
Celandine
Bilberry

CIRCULATION

Bayberry
Cayenne
Holy Thistle
(Blessed Thistle)
Butcher's Broom
Ginseng
Prickly Ash

COLDS & FLU (mixture)

Angelica
Cayenne
Cleavers
Elder Berry
Elder Flowers
Garlic
Horehound
Slippery Elm Bark Powder
Yarrow
Birch Bark
Chamomile
Coltsfood
Elecampane
Ginger
Hyssop
Vervain
Black Cohosh
Chickweed
Comfrey
Eucalyptus
Gum Arabic
Rose Hips
Wild Cherry Bark

CRAMPS

Alfalfa
Catnip
Bayberry Bark
Cramp Bark
Betony
Motherwort
Cohosh (black)
Blue Cohosh
Nettle

DIABETES

Blueberries and Leaf (Bilberry)
Peach Leaves
Uva Ursi
Cactus
Red Root
Yarrow

DIARRHEA

Chamomile or Camomile
Garlic
Meadowsweet
Elecampane
Ginger
St. Johnswort
Witch Hazel

EYE TROUBLE & WASH

Blueberries and leaf
Chamomile or Camomile
Sassafras
Brighan Tea
Eye Bright
Bilberry

FEMALE DOUCHE

Myrtle
Slippery Elm Bark Powder

FEVER

Cleaver's
Feverfew
Indian Hemp
Peppermint
Sage
Elder Flowers
Garlic
Pennyroyal (should not be use by
pregnant women)

GALL BLADDER TROUBLES

Birch
Corn Silk
Hops
Buchu
Dandelion Root
Kelp
Valerian Root
Pear Juice

GAS & INDIGESTION

Spearmint
Peppermint
Anise
Star Anise
Fennel
Fenugreek

GLAUCOMA

Bilberry

GOITER

Alfalfa
Dulse
Kelp

GOUT

Alfalfa
Chamomile
Buchu Leaves

Devil's Claw

HAY FEVER

Alfalfa
Blood Root
Bee Pollen
Coltsfoot
Eucalyptus

HEADACHES

Butcher's Broom
Hops
Skullcap
Blessed Thistle
Peppermint
St. Johnswort
White Willow Bark
Feverfew

HEART TROUBLES

Foxglove (Digitalis)
Blessed thistle
Hawthorn Berries
Lily of the Valley

HEMORRHOIDS

Alum Root
Chickweed
Burdock
Cranberry
Mullein

HIGH BLOOD PRESSURE

(Hypertension)

Barberry Bark or Root
Garlic
Mistletoe (European)
Red Clover
Valerian Root
Hawthorn Berries
Black Cohosh

IMPOTENCY (MALE)

Cayenne
Ginseng Root
Saw Palmetto Berries (Testes)
FoTi
Damiana
Sarsaparilla
Yohimbe

IMPOTENCY (FEMALE)

DongQuai
Ginseng (Siberian)

FoTi
Royal Jelly
False Unicorn

INSOMNIA

Catnip
Clovers
Passion Flower
Chamolie or Camomile
Hops
Skullcap
Valerian Root

INTERNAL HEMORRHAGE

Bayberry Bark
Bugle
Five Fingers
Passion Flower
Skullcap
Bistort
Comfrey
Golden Seal
Shepherd's Purse
Valerian Root

KIDNEY STONES OR TROUBLES

Black Cohosh (women)
Burdock
Juniper Berries
Parsley
Birch
Chamomile
Marshmallow

LAXATIVE

Aloes
Cascara Sagrada
Mandrake Root (small amount: ¼ of a teaspoon to ½ cup of water)
Buckthorn
Licorice Root
Senna Pods
Wahoo

LIVER DISORDERS

Angelica
Betony
Fennel
Ground Ivy
Agrimony
Balm
Dandelion
Fringe Tree (Jaundice)
Hops
Milk Thistle

MISCARRIAGES (Prevention)

Raspberry (Fruit & Juice)
Vitamin E 600 I.U. (Dry)
(dAlpha Tocopherol Succinate)
Wild Yams

MUCUS DECOMPOSER

Cayenne
Hyssop
Coughgrass
Sanicle
Wild Cherry Bark

NERVES

Borage
Chamomile
Hops
Mistletoe
Skullcap
Catnip
Cowslips
Ladies Slipper
Passion Flower
Valerian Root
*Mistletoe—*American will increase blood pressure
European will decrease blood pressure*

PREGNANCY

Motherwort
Spikenard
Raspberry Leaf
Squaw Vine

RHEUMATISM

Alfalfa
Cayenne
Boneset
Betony
Centuary
Sassafras
Birch
Devil's Claw
Wintergreen

SKIN TROUBLES

Aloe Vera
Centuary
Burdock
Elecampane
Solomon's Seal

SPLEEN TROUBLES

Angelica

Chamomile or Camomile
Ground Ivy
Balm
Gentian
Red Root

STIMULANTS

Angelica
Dandelion Root
Ginseng
Peppermint
Cayenne
Garlic
Onions
Yohimbe

STOMACH TROUBLES

Aloe Vera Juice
Comfrey
Golden Seal Root
Sage
Chamomile or Camomile
Ginger (Stomach Spasms)
Peppermint
Slippery Elm
Vervain

SWELLING

Balm
Ephedra
Mullein

TEETH & BREATH

Cayenne (apply to toothache)
Licorice Sticks (Licorice Root)
Pellitory (chew for toothache)
Clove
Myrrh Powder

THROAT TROUBLES

Bayberry
Golden Seal Powdered Root
Whole Ginger
Horehound
Fenugreek
Bee Proplolis

ULCERS

Comfrey
Olive Oil (extra virgin cold pressure)
Horsetail
Self Heal

VAGINAL INFECTIONS (Douche)

Golden Seal Root Powder
Myrtle
Slippery Elm Bark Power

VARICOSE VEINS

Cayenne
Marigold
White Oak (poultice)

VENEREAL DISEASES

Sarsaparilla
Sassafras
Witch Hazel Bark
Bee Propolis
Garlic

WEIGHT LOSS (OBESITY)

Buchu Leaves
Dandelion
Peach Bark
Seawrack
Chickweed
Fennel
Red Clover

WORMS

Black Walnut
Gentian Root
Mugwort
Sorrel
Garlic
Horehound
Plantain
Vervain
Sage

WOUNDS

Aloe Vera
Marigold
Comfrey
Self Heal

YEAST INFECTIONS

Acidophilus (nondairy)
Garlic
Caprylic Acid
Hydrogen Peroxide (food grade)

Gangrene
Alder

ULCERS
Anemone

Wounds

All Heal

Quinine Substitute
Antiseptics good in case of Leucorrhoea

Avens
Fever & Worms

Aspen
Encourages Sweating

Melissa
After Birth (Placenta), Nerves, Swelling
Balm

Cigarette Smoking, Depressant
Licorice Root
Laurel

Epileptics & Nervous Condition
Bedstraw

Minerals and Vitamin Sources of Herbs

VITAMIN A: Alfalfa, Burdock, Cayenne, Dandelion, Eye bright, Garlic, Kelp, Marshmallow, Okra Pods, Papaya, Paprika, Parsley, Pokeweed, Raspberry, Red Clover, Saffron, Spirulina, Watercress, Yellow Dock, Nettle

VITAMIN B_1: Cayenne, Chickweed, Dandelion, Fenugreek, Garlic, Kelp, Parsley, Raspberry, Yellow Dock

VITAMIN B_2: Alfalfa, Burdock, Dandelion, Fenugreek, Garlic, Kelp, Parsley, Raspberry, Saffron, Spirulina, Watercress

VITAMIN B_3: (Niacin) Alfalfa, Burdock, Dandelion, Fenugreek, Kelp, Parsley, Raspberry, Saffron, Spirulina

VITAMIN B_5: Alfalfa, Dandelion, Parsley, Wheat Grass

VITAMIN B_6: (Pyridoxine) Alfalfa, Spirulina, Nettle

VITAMIN B_{12}: (Cyanocobalamin; Cobalt) Alfalfa, Catnip, Comfrey, Dong Quai, Dulse, Kelp, Spirulina, nettle

VITAMIN B_{13}: (Pangamic Acid) Alfalfa, Comfrey, Dong Quai, Dulse, Kelp

VITAMIN B_{17}: Chaparral

VITAMIN C: Acerola, Alfalfa, Boneset, Burdock, Catnip, Cayenne, Chickweed, Dandelion, Garlic, Ground Ivy, Hawthorn, Horseradish, Kelp, Lobelia, Nettle, Papaya, Paprika, Parsley, Plantain, Pokeweed, Raspberry, Rose Hips, Shepherd's Purse, Strawberry, Watercress, Yellow Dock

VITAMIN D:	Alfalfa, Watercress
VITAMIN E:	Alfalfa, Dandelion, Kelp, Raspberry, Rose Hips, Spirulina, Watercress
VITAMIN F:	Burdock, Dandelion, Echinacea, Flaxseed, Kelp, Orris, Uva, Ursi
VITAMIN G:	Alfalfa, Cayenne, Dandelion, Gotu Kola, Kelp
VITAMIN H: (Biotin)	Alfalfa, Nettle
VITAMIN K:	Alfalfa, Plantain, Shepherd's Purse, Spirulina
VITAMIN P: (Rutin)	Dandelion, Rose Hips, Rue
VITAMIN T:	Plantain
VITAMIN U: (For Peptic Ulcers)	Alfalfa, Nettle
ALUMINUM:	Alfalfa, Nettle
CALCIUM:	Alfalfa, Arrowroot, Blue Cohosh, Camomile, Cayenne, Dandelion,. Irish Moss, Kelp, Mistle toe, Nettle, Parsley, Plantain, Pokeweed, Rasp berry, Rose Hips, Shepherd's Purse, Spirulina, Yellow Dock
CHLOROPHYLL:	Alfalfa, Spirulina, Nettle.
CHLORINE:	Alfalfa, Dandelion, Fennel, Kelp, Myrrh, Nettle, Parsley, Raspberry, Wheat Grass
COPPER:	Kelp, Parsley
FOLIC ACID:	Alfalfa, Dandelion, Garlic, Kelp, Parsley

FLUORINE: Garlic

INOSITOL: Alfalfa, Dandelion, Kelp, Nettle, Parsley, Wheat Grass

IODINE: Dulse, Garlic, Irish Moss, Kelp, Sarsaparilla Nori, Spirulina

IRON: Alfalfa, Burdock, Blue Cohosh, Cayenne, Dandelion, Dulse, Kelp, Mullein, Nettle, Nori, Parsley, Pokeweed, Rhubarb, Rose Hips, Yellow Dock, Raspberry, Yohimbe

LITHIUM: Kelp, Spirulina

MAGNESIUM: Alfalfa, Blue Cohosh, Cayenne, Dandelion, Kelp, Mistletoe, Mullein, Peppermint, Primrose, Raspberry, Willow, Wintergreen

MANGANESE: Kelp, Spirulina

PHOSPHORUS: Alfalfa, Blue Cohosh, Caraway, Cayenne, Chickweed, Dandelion, Garlic, Irish Moss, Kelp, Licorice, Parsley, Purslane, Pokewood, Raspberry, Rose Hips, Watercress, Yellow Dock,

POTASSIUM: Alfalfa, Blue Cohosh, Birch, Borage, Camomile, Coltsfoot, Comfrey, Centaury, Dandelion, Dulse, Eyebright, Fennel, Irish Moss, Kelp, Mistletoe, Mullein, Nettle, Papaya, Parsley, Peppermint, Plantain, Primrose, Raspberry, Shepherd's Purse, White Oak Bark, Wintergreen, Yarrow

SELENIUM: Kelp, Spirulina

SILICON: Alfalfa, Blue Cohosh, Burdock, Horsetail, Kelp, Nettle

SODIUM: Alfalfa, Dandelion, Dulse, Eyebright, Fennel, Irish Moss, Kelp, Mistletoe, Parsley, Shepherd's

Purse, Spirulina, Willow

SULFUR: Alfalfa, Burdock, Cayenne, Coltsfoot, Eyebright, Fennel, Garlic, Irish Moss, Kelp, Mullein, Nettle, Parsley, Plantain, Raspberry, Sage, Shepherd's Purse, Thyme

ZINC: Kelp, Marshmallow

TRACE Minerals:
Dulse, Kelp, Nori, Spirulina
(Boron, Bromine, Nickel, Strontium, Vanadium)

NUTS AND SEEDS

1. Best nut is the almond without the skin.
2. Filberts are good
3. Sunflower seeds are excellent
4. Sesame seeds are excellent
5. Pumpkin seeds are excellent (hulled)
6. Flax seeds are excellent
7. Milk thistle seeds
8. Walnuts
9. Chia seeds are excellent

Herbal Tips

HERBS THAT CONTAIN HORMONES:

Black Cohosh (natural estrogen). Women would benefit most from this herb. Helps in Menopause.

Licorice Root (natural cortisone). Beneficial to women and men. For coughs and chest complaints, gastric ulcers, throat conditions, hoarseness and Asthma. Sarsaparilla (all the hormones). Here's one for the men. Contains testosterone (male hormone) in organic form.

DIURETIC HERBS:

Damiana	Watermelon Seeds
Chamomile or Camomile	Fennel Seed
Buchu Leaves	Parsley
	Uva Ursi

TIPS:

1. Dandelion root destroys acids in the blood.

2. Comfrey root is the best remedy for blood in the urine.

3. Chickweed is one of the best remedies for tumors, piles, swollen testes, ulcerated throat and mouth and deafness.

4. Cornsilk is an excellent remedy for inflammatory conditions of the urethra, bladder and kidneys. Cornsilk is also a good source to prevent bedwetting.

5. Horsetail (shavegrass) is an important agent to cleanse your body of lead.

HERBS TO COMBAT VIRUSES

Astragalus	Barley Green
Pycnogenol	Rose Hips

6. Kelp reduces radioactive strontium 90.

7. Peach bark is very good for morning sickness.

8. Psyllium seed is called the colon broom because it cleans out compacted pockets in the colon.

9. Red raspberry helps to prevent miscarriage.

10. Yarrow if taken freely at the beginning of a cold will break it up in 24 hours.

11. Morning Sickness:

Motherwort	Red Raspberry
Queen of Meadow	Rose Hips

FLOWER POLLEN

FLOWER POLLEN

1. What is flower pollen?

Pollen is created when plants produce flowers. It is the
male germ seed of plants. Pollination occurs when the
pollen is carried by bees, wind or other means from the
flower's stamen to the stigma of another flower's pistil.
Fertilization occurs when the pollen reaches the ovary.
This is when a seed is created. Without this process there
wouldn't be any plant life on earth flowers, fruits, vegetables, trees, etc. Pollen is microscopic. So small, it would
take almost 10,000 pollen grains to cover the size of your
thumbnail. Each grain has an almost impenetrable outer
shell. On the inside of the shell is where the nutrients are
found. Think of a seed (such as sunflower seed) that has
an outer shell with the 'meat' or nutrients inside. Each
pollen grain has tiny germinal openings called hilas. These
openings are used by the seed to bring forth sprouts. Bees
collect flower pollen, then bring it back to the hive. Bees
use special enzymes to get through the hard outer shells
and remove the nutrient rich insides. Bees use this nutri-
tive substance to make honey, royal jelly, Propolis, and
other materials used in the hive.

2. What is the difference between bee pollen and flower pollen?

Flower pollen (as sold by LE TAN) is just the inside nutrients not the outer shell. Bee pollen (as sold around the
world) is the whole pollen grain outer shell included. When
you eat bee pollen it is like eating walnuts or pecans. Even
though you have digestive enzymes secreted by the pancreas they couldn't fully break down the outer shells to
get to the nutrient rich nut inside. You would then excrete
the walnuts or pecans fully intact. Little or no nutrients
would have been absorbed into your system. Eating flower
pollen, on the other hand, would be like eating just the
nut inside of a walnut or pecan hard outer shell removed.
Your system would get full benefit of the nutrient rich nut.
Here are two other differences. First Bees collect pollen

from any flower they want to. They then go through man-made traps that scrape the pollen off their legs into a container (we feel this to be unkind). These traps can be contaminated by fungus, bacteria, insect eggs, mites, rodent hair, droppings, and debris, as well as other contaminates. LE TAN's flower pollen is gathered by hand in Spain from pollution free, pest free, chemical free (NO weed killers or fertilizers) fields of specially grown plants. Bees don't have this quality control since they go anywhere they want: to fields that were chemically treated or to flowers that an animal had sprayed a scent marking on, etc.

Second. Since bee pollen contains the hard outer shell, people can be allergic to it. These outer shells have ridges all over them which is what makes you sneeze and have teary eyes when you come in contact with pollen through the air. Since flowers pollen doesn't contain the outer shell it is allergy free.

3. Why should I take flower pollen?

Since flower pollen contains nearly every known nutrient to man, and without a doubt every nutrient needed to sustain plant life it must be considered the purest possible food. Since the beginning of time (even God said it in Genesis 1:29) flower pollen is the perfect food source. There is no 'multivitamin' on the market today that contains the hundreds of substances found in flower pollen. Most only contain 20 to 30 nutrients. And nearly all (and we mean over 90%) of the vitamins manufactured today are chemical synthetics. This means even though they are labeled 'natural' (which most companies do) they are made from petroleum (yes the !stuff' that comes out of the ground and we use for oil and gas). From petroleum it is synthesized into molecular structures and then used as vitamins. We consider these 'vitamins' dead, (bioactively dead), not 'natural,' not bonded to enzymes like nutrients found in food, etc. We feel these 'multivitamins' pale in comparison to the truly all organic, flower pollen. There are a few companies (out of hundreds), that 'grow' algae or microscopic plants in stainless steel drums and are truly natural vitamins. Yet flower pollen is organic and contains many times more nutrients than even these 'multivitamins' do. And we as nutritionists, believe that the body needs every one of these nutrients found in flower pollen to sustain a healthy life. We also believe when your body is robbed of these nutrients that some very bad things happen. One of dozens of examples would be: when the body doesn't get all the nutrients it needs it signals the brain to have hunger pains. This causes a person to be hungry, because of which they eat more food. This continues as a vicious circle, which is a major factor to obesity.

4. Who takes flower pollen?

Everybody! But especially anyone who has an understanding of body functions and nutritional research on flower pollen.

Like:

A) Bodybuilders. In an article by Dr. G.K. Knowlton entitled "Steroids—There are Natural Alternatives to Anabolic Substances" (in the Jan. 86 issue of Exercise For Men Only Magazine), he said this about flower pollen, "Flower pollen, NOT bee pollen, in Europe, this is regarded as almost a miracle substance. Double blind European medical studies have suggested that this substance will have a moderate but significantly preventive effect on the common cold, improve athletic performance in weightlifters, and have a slight effect on the healing time of bone fractures. It is used extensively in athletics and especially in endurance oriented sports."

B) Movie stars and famous personalities. It is rumored that a famous nutritionist introduced our former President to flower pollen, and that he has used it faithfully for dozens of years. Many famous people have come out publicly stating the benefits of flower pollen.

C) Professional sports athletes and Gold Medal Olympians. Our only competition (Cernitin America), has used many names in association/promotion with their company. Such as: Bob McAdoo (who said he was using flower pollen when the Lakers won the NBA Championship), Bill Walton, Curly Neal, and Oscar Robertson. Nine time world powerlifting champion Larry Pacifico. Olympic gymnasts: Julianne McNamara, Nadia Comaneci, coach Bela

Karolyi, and Mary Lou Retton. Mr. USA Bodybuilding champ Gary Strydom. Boxer Muhammed Ali. and only player to win two Heismann trophies Archie Griffin.

5. Why LE TAN's Flower Pollen?

Most importantly, because LE TAN (Life Extension Today's Advanced Nutrition) is a nutritional company, NOT a fly-by-night car salesman type of vitamin manufacturer. We take years of research from the most notable, major, and reputable laboratories and agencies in the world to formulate our products, including flower pollen. Our flower pollen comes from the sunny country of Spain. The climate is perfect, the air is clean, the ground is not contaminated, the plants are healthy, the environment is pure, etc. Our pollen is pure, contains no animal products, preservatives, or man-made chemicals.

6. How much flower pollen should I take?

We recommend 3 or more tablets daily. One or more with each meal. If you are feeling tired or 'down' in the mid-afternoon, take a couple of tablets with a glass of water for a 'nutritious snack.' Before working out, exercise, or any activity, you can take 3 to 5 tablets for an endurance booster.

Each tablet contains 250 mg. of pure flower pollen. There are 100 tablets per bottle.

"And God said, 'Behold, I have given you every herb bearing seed which is upon the face of all the earth, and every tree, in which is the fruit of a tree yielding seed (pollen); to you it shall be for food.' " Genesis 1:29

A PARTIAL CHEMICAL ESSAY OF LE TAN'S
FLOWER POLLEN

VITAMINS
Provitamin A
B_1 Thiamine
B_2 Riboflavin
Niacin
B_6 Pyridoxine
Pantothenic Acid
Biotin
B_{12}
Folic Acid
Vitamin C
Vitamin D
Vitamin E
Vitamin K

MINERALS
Boron
Calcium
Chlorine
Chromium
Copper
Iodine
Iron
Magnesium
Manganese
Molybdenum
Phosphorus
Potassium
Silicon
Sodium
Sulphur
Titanium
Zinc

FLAVINOIDS
Apigenin
Dihydrokaempferol
Dihydroxquercetin
Isorhamnetin
Kaempferol
Luteolin
Myricetin
Naringenin
Quercetin
Rutin

GROWTH REGULATORS
Auxins
Brassins
Gibberellins
Kinins

AMINO ACIDS
Alanine
AlphaAminoButyric Acid
Arginine
Asparagine
Aspartic Acid
Cysteine
Cystine Gluatamic Acid Glutamine
Glycine, Histidine
Hydroxyproline
Isoleucine, Leucine
Lysine Methionine
Phenylalanine
Proline, Serine,
Thereonine,
Tryptophan Tyrosine
Valine

FATTY ACIDS
Caprylic
Capric
Lauric
Myristic
Myristoleic
Pentadecanoic
Palmitic
Palmitoleic
Heptadecanoic
Stearic
Oleic
Linoleic
Linolenic
Arachidic
Eicosenoic
Eicosadienoic
Eicosatrienoic
Arachidonic

CAROTENOIDS

Betacarotene
Xanthophylls (including
Canthaxanthin)
Zeaxanthin
Lycopene
Crocetin

LIPIDS

Lecithin
Lysolecithin
Phosphotidyl
Inositol
Phosphatidylcholine
Monoglycerides
Diglycerides
Triglycerides
Free fatty acids
Sterols
Hydrocarbons

SUGARS

Arabinose
Fructose
Fucose
Galactose
Glucoronolactone
Glucose
Hexasamine
Maltose
Maltotetratose
Maltotriose
Mannose
Raffinose
Rhamnose
Ribose
Stachyose
Sucrose
Xylitole
Xylogalacturonan
Xylose

PHTOSTEROLS

Fucosterol
Betasitosterol
Stigmasterol
Campesterol
Estrone

HYDROCARBONS

npentacosane
nheptacosane
nnonacosane ntricosane
myoinositol, Pinitol
Sequitol

Amines
Chlorophyll
Guanine
Hexodecanal
Hypoxalthine
Nuclein
Nucleosides
Nucleic Acids
Pentosans
Phenolic Acids
Tarpenes
Vernine
Xanthine

ENZYMES
CLASS

Transferases
Aspartate carbamoyltransferase
alpha Glucanphosphorylase,
Penzyme Maltose
4glucosyltransferase
amylomaltase
UDPGlucosebetaglucan
glucosyltransferase
TrehalosephosphateUDP
glucosyltransferase
alphaGlucanbranching
glycosyltransferase
UDPGalactoseglucose
galactosyltransferase
Aspartate aminotransferase
Glycine aminotransferase
Hexokinase Glucokinase
Xylulokinase
Phosphoribulokinase
Glucuronokinase
Nucleosidediphosphate kinase
Phosphoglucomutase
DNA Nucleotidyltransferase
UDPGlucose pyrophosphorylase
ADPGlucose pyrophosphorylase
Ribonuclease

CLASS

Hydrolases
Carboxylesterase
Arylesterase
Lipase
Cutinase
Pectinesterase
Alkaline phosphatase
Acid phoshatase
Phytase, Trehalosephosphatase,
Phosphodieterase
Deoxyribonuclease

Arylsuphatase
alpha-Amylase
beta-Amylase
Cellulase, Laminaranase,
Polygalacturonase
alpha-Glucosidase
beta-Glucosidase
alpha-Mannosidase
beta-Fructofuranosidase,
Invertase
Trehalase
beta-N-Acetyglucosaminidase
Oligol, 3-glucosidase
Leucine aminopeptiadase
Aminopeptidase
Pepsin, Protease
Trypsin
Aminoacylase
Inorganic pyrophosphatase
ATPase

CLASS

Lyases
Pyruvic decarbosylase
Oxaloacetat decarboxylase
Mesoxalic decarboxylase
Glutamic decarboxylase
Phosphopyruvate carboxylase
Ribulosediphosphate carboxylase,
          carboxydismutase
Ketose-l-phosphate aldolase
Fructosediphosphate aldolase
Citrate synthase
Phenylalanine ammoinialyase

CLASS

Isomerases
UDPGlucose epimerase
Arabinose isomerase
Xylose isomerase
Ribosephosphate isomerase
Glucosephosphate isomerage

BEE PROPOLIS

NO ALCOHOL, NO CHEMICAL SOLVENT

PROPOLIS

RAW, NATURAL, ORGANIC

Propolis is a resinous substance gathered by the bees from the leaf buds or the bark of poplars, chestnuts and other common trees . The bees then use the propolis as a "cement" that lines the walls of the hive in which they prepare honey, pollen, royal jelly and other related byproducts. Nature has provided bees with this substance to keep them and their hives free of germs in spite of 40,000 to 50,000 bees being crammed into close quarters in the hive.

Researchers around the world are hailing its powers. So far they say it has helped:

Cancer. Dr. Mitja Vosnjak, former deputy minister of foreign in Yugoslavia, reported at a medical conference that a friend dying of stomach cancer was told to take ¼ teaspoon of proplis three times a day.

Within a few days, the patient had "no pains, no cramps and no bleeding. "After six weeks he was gaining weight and the cancer seemed to be in remission.

Ulcers. Dr. Franz Klemens Feiks of Austria reported: "We gave a dose of ½teaspoon before meals, three times a day. The group taking propolis showed pain disappeared within three days in seven of 10 cases." "After 10 days no wounds could be detected in six of 10 patients."

Influenza . In Sarajevo, Yugoslavia. Professor Izet Osmanagic tested volunteers who were exposed to influenza. Eighty-eight patients took propolis 182 did not.

Only seven percent on propolis got the flu, while 63 percent of the others contracted it.

Along with the ailments listed above, propolis has also been known to help:

****

Sore lips and gums	Respiratory distress
Blemishes or bruises	Broken bones
Burns	Colds and related ailments
Sore throat	Skin healing
Skin blemishes	Better physical strength
Nasal congestion	Influenza

****

The greenish to brownish glue-like material with an aromatic smell and slightly bitter taste is made up of 50 to 55 percent resin and balsam, 30 percent wax and eight to 10 percent pollen.
Some researchers think the therapeutic properties of propolis come from substances called flavonoids, found in the resin. It is rich in minerals, B vitamins and antibiotics and works to raise the body's natural resistance by stimulating it to produce its own disease fighting defenses.

Bees collect propolis, treat it with their own enzymes and use the sticky material to patch holes or cracks in the hive.

This organic 'cement' protects the insects and their home from contamination, moisture and germs.

"The bees have relied on it for 46 million years," says Dr. Kupsinel, a Florida physician. "The bees must be doing something right because beehives contain less bacteria and are more sterile that hospitals," says Dr. Kupsinel.

References

(l) Ross, R. The Globe (March 25, 1980) Pg. 5

(2) Wade, C. Propolis: Nature's Energizer (1983) Keats Publishing, INC.

****

Y.S. GENUINE PROPOLIS IS ABSOLUTELY GUARANTEED

****

* THE CHOICE PROPOLIS (THE BEST !) % CORE PORTION)

* NO ALCOHOL, NO CHEMICAL SOLVENT EVER USED

* SAFE, CLEAN, FULL POTENCY

* NEW, FRESH CROPS DIRECT FROM BEEKEEPERS

BEAUTY HINTS

Although wise respectable women do not expose their bodies publicly, some have been left marred by the wonderful event of child birth. Diligent use of Vitamin E oil on stretch marks or skin blemishes of any kind may greatly diminish or eventually completely eradicate such marks. Application to face, neck, elbows, and knees make them smooth and soft without blemishes.

A natural, organic nail file in the form of fish scales is available in most health food stores. This valuable item can not only be used for manicuring but it's a necessary adjunct to the sister who desires soft and attractive feet. This file may be used to erase corns and calluses. Since the feet are sexy to most males, they should be pedicured regularly and kept pretty and odor free.

BATHS

Allure and fascinate your mate with a natural, refreshing herbal bath. Fill a piece of cheese cloth with $1/2$ cup of either mixture of the following herbs: Strawberry leaf, spearmint, peppermint, orange leaves, camomile, sage, rosemary, pennyroyal, rose buds or lavender, comfrey.

Drop into a warm bath and let soak for 15 minutes. Add a few drops of natural bath oil, immerse your body(s) and enjoy a fragrant and refreshing, relaxing, rejuvenating bath.

NATURAL DEODORANT

In case of allergy to commercial deodorants, a mixture of corn starch, lemon juice, and baking soda makes a very effective underarm deodorant.

NATURAL BREATH FRESHENER

Pour boiling water on a portion of a mixture of peppermint, spearmint leaves and fennel seeds. Add a few drops of liquid chlorophyll. Store in refrigerator. Use daily as needed.

It has been established that cow's milk, being formulated by nature for calves, those weight is 300 times that of a human infant, is unsuitable for babies of African descendant. The high content of the element casein makes it difficult for the infant to burp or expel the air created by swallowing while nursing and in some cases, cause the infant to die. Thus, heretofore, unexplained deaths have 'been labeled "Crib Death."

DRY BRUSH MASSAGE

Dry brush massage for the entire body, using a natural bristle brush. Use twice a day.

DISEASES

DISEASES MORE PREVALENT IN AFRICAN PEOPLE VIS-A-VIS CAUCASIANS

DISEASE	MEN	WOMEN
ANEURYSMS:	Swollen blood vessels in the brain	
BLOOD PRESSURE (Hypertension)		Known as the "silent killer," Black women are beset by this disease more often than men—30% women, 28% men. Corrective Measures: ■ No smoking, reduce stress, less salt in diet and food low in cholesterol and fat.

DISEASE	MEN	WOMEN
CANCER	810% higher in Africans (meaning Black people or non-whites) than found in whites. Cancer was most often found in the uterus/cervical, breasts, and lungs. The death rate is up 25% in Blacks. Causes may be environmental, but most probably due to poorer nutritional practice.	
BREAST CANCER		Highest in Black Women
UTERUS CANCER		Highest in Black Women
LUNG CANCER	Highest in Afrikan American Community	
DIABETES		Higher amongst African women, yet black men and women surpass whites in this category.
HEART DISEASE	Heart Attacks	Angina
LUPUS		Highest among black women
PROSTATE CANCER	Highest among Black Men	
STRESS RELATED	Alcoholism	Cigarette Smoking
TUBERCULOSIS	Highest among	Black men
OBESITY	Highest in African American Community	

ENVIRONMENTAL TOXINS

ENVIRONMENTAL TOXINS

MICROWAVE OVENS:

1. Electromagnetic forces on the body causes free radicals. Microwave ovens destroy the molecular components of amino acids in foods. The enzymes that are the catalysis for life are lost when food is "nuked."

TELEVISION & VDT

■ Color television viewing/contact should be at least 4–6 feet away from the television.

■ Video Displayed Terminals (VDT): Emit electromagnetic radiation.

■ Florescent lights are toxic—nervous system. Full spectrum lights are better.

■ Digital Clocks offset the body's electric senses—electromagnetic pulses can offset magnetic pulses in the body—they adversely affect energy and oxygen.

OTHER ENVIRONMENTAL TOXICOSIS:

* Improper Ventaliation

■ Basement—Bacteria, Viruses. Mold Spores, Fungus

■ Uncleaned Air Conditioners breed diseases or ventilation systems (water systems are better)

■ Bathrooms must have vents to prevent mold or bacteria spores; windows also are necessary in bathrooms.

■ Carpets have formaldehyde

■ Chemicals in furniture

■ Pets bring mites (carpet mites get into your eyes, and hair)

■ Bed Linen: Sheets should be untreated all cotton. Do not use bleach in your laundry—Ivory Snow is the best commercial detergent, or Dr. Bronner's Peppermint soap.

■ Bed mattresses contain harmful chemicals to the body, and allergic reaction—mattresses that are chemical free, and that have natural fibers are best.

■ Toilet paper that is colored is not good for anal wipes, for the chemical dyes in toilet paper are irritants to the anus. White soft untreated toilet paper is the best.

■ Toothbrushes should be changed once every three to four weeks. Bacteria and germs build up very fast on toothbrushes.

■ Gargle with hydrogen peroxide.

Bibliography

1) Africa, Llaila 0. 1983, 1989 "African Holistic Health" abesegun, Johnson, and Koram Publishers Silver Springs Maryland 20904

2) Balch, James F. M.D. and Balch, Phyllis A., C.N.C. 1990 "Prescription for Nutritional Healing " Avery Publishing Group Garden City Park, New York

3) Bernard, R.W. A.B., M.A., Ph D 1956 "The Organic Way to Health" Health Research Mokelumne Hill, California

4) Heritage, Ford 1968 "Composition and Facts about Foods" Health Research Mokelumne Hill, California 95245

5) Hoffman, Jay Milton, Ph D. 1981, 1982 "The Missing Link In the Medical Curriculum" Professional Press Publishing Company Valley Center, Calif, 92082

6) Kirschmann, John D. 1973 "Nutrition Almanac" Nutrition Search Minneapolis, Minnesota 55402

7) Law, Donald Ph D. 1972 Herbs for Cooking and Healing" Wilshire Book Company No. Hollywood, California 91605

8) Null, Gary 1987 "The Egg Project" Four Walls Eight Windows Village Station, New York, N.Y. 10014